ALSO BY TANYA SELVARATNAM

*The Big Lie: Motherhood, Feminism,
and the Reality of the Biological Clock*

ASSUME NOTHING

ASSUME NOTHING

A Memoir of Intimate Violence

TANYA
SELVARATNAM

HENRY HOLT AND COMPANY

NEW YORK

Henry Holt and Company
Publishers since 1866
120 Broadway
New York, New York 10271
www.henryholt.com

Henry Holt ® and 🏛® are registered trademarks of Macmillan
Publishing Group, LLC.

Library of Congress Cataloging-in-Publication Data is available.

ISBN: 9781250214249

Our books may be purchased in bulk for promotional,
educational, or business use. Please contact your local
bookseller or the Macmillan Corporate and Premium Sales
Department at (800) 221-7945, extension 5442, or by email at
MacmillanSpecialMarkets@macmillan.com.

First Edition 2020

Designed by Meryl Sussman Levavi

Printed in the United States of America

10 9 8 7 6 5 4 3 2 1

For everyone who shared their stories and compelled me to write this book

To withhold words is power. But to share our words with others, openly and honestly, is also power.

—Terry Tempest Williams, *When Women Were Birds*

CONTENTS

ASSUME NOTHING

INTRODUCTION

Early in our relationship, he told me that he could tap my phone and have me followed. Because he was the attorney general of New York, I knew Eric Schneiderman had the power to do this. His power was a thread that ran throughout our relationship. Over the course of about a year, I was broken down by the slapping, spitting, and choking that he inflicted on me during sex, never with my consent, and by his gaslighting, which destroyed my self-esteem.

"Don't be afraid. Don't be ashamed," I told myself every day in the months before my story of abuse became public. I had decided to come forward after I realized I was part of a pattern. It wasn't just my story; other women shared it. And I had to tell it to help prevent still others from having it become their story, too.

In early January 2018, I spoke with David Remnick, editor of the *New Yorker*, about my experience with Schneiderman. I gave Remnick my word that I wouldn't talk to other publications while he decided how to proceed. He told me that if I were alone in coming forward, I would be in peril.

On March 20, my birthday, *New Yorker* staff writer Jane Mayer called me at Remnick's request, wanting to hear about my experience in my own words. After hearing me describe it in great detail, Mayer echoed Remnick's opinion: if I were alone in coming forward, I would be in peril. She asked me to give her time while she tried to contact other previous girlfriends of Schneiderman. Within two weeks, she had spoken with two, and their stories were eerily similar to mine.

At that point, I knew that the story's coming out was inevitable. I also knew that despite being terrified, I had to participate on the record to give it weight. Moreover, I knew deep down that I was doing the right thing, and I had clear objectives: to warn other women about him and to highlight the hypocrisy of men who claim to be champions of women publicly but abuse them privately.

Eric would often say, "Assume nothing." He would also say, "Trust no one." In my relationship with Eric, I went through the classic stages that structure intimate partner violence, stages that almost all victims go through: entrapment, isolation, control, demeaning, and abuse. My story is a testament to what survivors of intimate partner violence experience, how long it can take even a feminist like me to recognize and name the abuse, and how we can get out, get help, and advocate for more awareness and solutions.

When Rachael Denhollander, Aly Raisman, and the Sister Army of gymnasts spoke out about abuse by the doctor Larry Nassar, they ended a cycle. When Olympic soccer medalist Hope Solo spoke out about the sexual assault she had experienced by former FIFA president Sepp Blatter, she changed the perception of what a victim looks like. In speaking out, I was determined to present my own behavior, as humiliating as the details were. I was making myself vulnerable in a way I didn't want to be, when it would have been far easier to move on and do nothing. I would much rather have gone on with my life and not gotten caught up in the mess of coming forward. But if ever there was a moment to come forward, I saw, this was the time, against the backdrop of #MeToo and #TimesUp. Intimate partner violence education can empower victims to spot it and get out of it. I hope that by telling my story, contextualizing it with other people's stories, and offering advice from experts, I can do my part to change the conversation and outcomes around this issue.

After the New Yorker article came out, I worked hard to understand how I got into a relationship with a man who made me feel so bad about myself. I had a long bridge to cross before I could be in an intimate relationship again.

I spent a lot of time studying and understanding the tactics of abusers. According to the National Coalition Against Domestic Violence, on average, nearly twenty people per minute are physically abused by an intimate partner in the United States. In one year, this equates to more than ten million women and men. The demographics of both abusers and victims cut across racial, economic, and religious lines.

The cycle of violence that permeates every aspect of our lives is an existential and, in many cases, mortal threat to our shared humanity. Through it, we become conditioned to accept violence as part of our day-to-day lives. It's up to us to end the cycle. Tarana Burke said about the Me Too movement she started in 2006, "I feel that one of the strongest pathways to healing is releasing your story, and then doing the work required to begin to heal." I hope that by writing this book, I will help others—to share their own stories, to support loved ones in abusive relationships, and even to avoid becoming a victim.

I wish I didn't have memories of being a victim myself. No one wants such memories. But I feel that somehow the universe intended for me, through these events, to encounter Eric Schneiderman and, eventually, end a cycle with his intimate partners that had been going on for a long time.

CHAPTER 1

THE FAIRY TALE

We met in July 2016, at the Democratic National Convention in Philadelphia. Producing election-related videos in 2016 was my first step into electoral politics. It wasn't work I had sought to do, but when I was approached about the opportunity, I didn't hesitate. I wanted to get involved because I recognized the danger that the Republican candidate, Donald Trump, posed to America. As soon as he announced he was running, I thought, "This crook is going to win." And I felt that if I didn't contribute to the effort to stop him, I wouldn't be able to sleep at night.

Prior to 2016, I had been more likely to be at an art opening, book signing, or theater show. It wasn't normal for me to attend large-scale political events, but that was my life at the time.

As for that first fateful encounter with Eric Schneiderman, I hadn't planned to be in the spot where he introduced himself to me. I hadn't planned to be at the convention at all that night. After a long day producing a film shoot, I had wanted to stay in. But a series of unexpected events led to our meeting anyway.

It began with a friend who was on the finance committee for Hillary Clinton's campaign texting me that he had an extra pass. He was going to leave it with the receptionist at his hotel if I wanted it. I thought, "Why not?" Then, while on the subway, I received a message from a friend I'd emailed with the day before that he could see through Facebook that I was nearing the convention center. I texted him when I arrived, and he brought me to where he was sitting. It turned out to be the box of Ed Rendell, the former governor of Pennsylvania.

While I was perched on a stool, taking notes, I could feel a man glancing at me. I turned to my right and smiled at him. I was wearing a cobalt-blue dress with stars, a white vest, and red shoes. I must have looked like a proud American. He walked over.

"You're *writing* notes," he said, surprised.

Others around me were on their phones or laptops, but I was using a notebook and pen.

Tim Kaine, the vice presidential candidate, was speaking. The man said he had gone to Harvard Law School with Kaine. I said that I had gone to Harvard for undergrad and grad.

"What did you study?"

"Chinese language and the history of law," I replied.

He asked, in Chinese, "Do you speak Chinese?"

I responded, in Chinese, "Yes, but I can't speak fluently anymore."

It was a charming and nerdy flirtation. He asked if I knew who he was. I did not.

"Where do you live?"

"New York," I said.

"Then I'm your lawyer."

He was surprised I didn't know who he was. His name was Eric Schneiderman, and he was the attorney general of New York State.

After he walked away to rejoin his group, I found myself thinking about him. I was curious and wanted to know more about him. I thought he was handsome. I wondered if I would see him again. I wanted to.

The next night, I was back at the convention and seated in a section high above the floor. I could see Eric on the Jumbotron as the cameras panned over to where he stood with the New York delegation on the floor. I realized then that he was a big deal. During the proceedings, he and I were emailing back and forth. We wouldn't see each other that night, but he said he would call me the next day. I decided to have no expectations. Maybe he would, maybe he wouldn't.

After the convention, I got a ride back to New York with Carrie Mae Weems, an artist I'd worked with for many years who had become a close friend. While we were in the car, he did in fact call. I felt butterflies. I was excited, and Carrie was excited for me, too. I was also impressed that he did what he had said he was going to do. So many times, I had been disappointed by men not doing so—not calling, or canceling at the last minute, as if I had nothing better to do than wait for them.

Eric and I made plans to meet for lunch the next day. He came downtown so that it would be convenient for me, and he told his security detail that he didn't need them to accompany us.

He seemed nervous when we met up. Abruptly, he said,

"I haven't vetted you yet," which seemed a strange thing to say right off the bat. I could feel a spark between us, but his comment took me out of the moment. I thought to myself, "Well, I've been vetted recently by the Hillary campaign."

That night I was leaving for Portland, Oregon, for three weeks. He was going to a meditation retreat upstate.

Later, he sent me articles about himself, one from the *American Prospect* about him being "the man the banks fear most" and one from the *Nation* by him about "transforming the liberal checklist." We stayed in contact through occasional emails, getting to know each other.

Once, he wrote, "I am up in the woods with little reception, but will loop back in upon my return to the wheel of samsara. I hope you are well."

It was an optimistic time both in terms of our interactions with each other and in terms of the outlook for the election. But I was bewildered that he seemed interested in me. I didn't feel I looked like a politician's type. I thought I looked too unconventional; I rarely got my hair done, and in my daily life, even at work, I could wear what I wanted. I wasn't the kind to be seen in monochromatic A-line dresses and pumps.

He emailed me when he was back in the city and sent a brief about Exxon, with whom he was engaged in a legal battle. He was a hero of the climate change movement. Two days later, he sent another article about himself and another battle, this one with Trump.

"Good fantasy reading before bed . . ." he wrote.

Although I could have been put off by his boasting, I saw it as a sign that he was trying to impress me. I felt flattered. I also felt that I could not reciprocate. What would I send him?

An article on my book about my infertility struggles? A review of a downtown theater show I'd been in?

The night I returned to New York, he sent me yet another article about Exxon and wrote "Calling!" But I was at a friend's birthday dinner and told him I'd call afterward. For the next few days, he rang me every night, and we spoke for an hour or more. Then he asked me out to dinner.

I arrived at the restaurant before him. When he got there, he was buoyant, almost dancing. His favorite jazz song was playing. During dinner, he joked about my being a spy sent by Exxon and said that they had done a very good job. Soon, though, his expression grew dark, and he said, "You know, I could have your phone tapped." He also said he could have me followed. Was he trying to impress me? Was he trying to scare me? The moment passed in an instant, and I let it go. Otherwise, he was sweet and attentive, curious about my life and my work.

We didn't go home together. Later that night, he sent another article about Exxon. He also sent me a photo of him with Ram Dass, the spiritual teacher and author of *Be Here Now*.

And he sent his "Transformational Activism Memo," which he said he had cowritten but which had been put out under the name of his friend, a meditation teacher. The memo provided a conceptual framework to "combine personal transformation with social and political activism aimed at transforming society."

The following week, he invited me to join him in Amagansett, where his law school buddy had a home. Eric was waiting for me at the jitney stop wearing a blue short-sleeved polo shirt and jeans. I was wearing a summer dress with a watermelon print. I immediately felt like we were on vacation together. Back at the house, we had separate rooms, but they were next to each other. That night, after dinner, we made love. Then he wanted to look at the moonlight, so we went outside, onto the balcony. He wanted to dance and brought out a portable speaker. He held me gently and looked into my eyes as if he couldn't believe I was there.

The next day, he took me to two fundraisers for Hillary Clinton in private homes. At the first one, everyone I met on Hillary's team seemed to know who I was. I took it as normal protocol that they had been briefed in advance about my background, specifically that I was volunteering as a producer of videos in support of the campaign. I was brought into a closed-off area where people were lined up to meet Hillary. When Eric and I finally got to her, she seemed keen to talk to him. After all, he was the greatest hope for keeping her opponent in check. Moreover, if she won, Eric would be primed to play a central role in enacting her policies in New York State. Later, when she addressed the crowd, she name checked Eric and complimented him on the work he was doing.

At the second fundraiser, Harvey Weinstein was one of the first people to approach Eric. He wanted to help him raise money, saying that Eric was "the only guy doing anything." I didn't know what to make of Weinstein. I had friends who worked for him. I had heard years before that he would make his assistants procure drugs and prostitutes for him when he was at film festivals. But here, at this event, he was with his daughter and seemed to dote on her.

Bill Clinton was seated near us. He looked over to Eric and said he wanted to ask him something before he left. I saw a woman I knew and wanted to say hello. Eric said about this woman and her husband, who were big philanthropists, "Oh, they don't give me money." He didn't say it maliciously, but I was gathering that at events like these, someone like him had to focus on his supporters—that he didn't have time for anyone else. I went to say hi to her anyway.

At the end of the night, Bill and Eric connected. Eric introduced Bill to me. Bill shook my hand firmly and wouldn't let it go while he asked Eric for advice about the Clinton Foundation and fundraising, wanting to know when they needed to stop taking foreign donations. Eric gave him his card and said that someone in his office would help answer any questions. I was stunned by the overtness of the interaction, but it also emphasized that Eric was an influential man.

A few days later, while we were still in Amagansett, Eric asked if I'd come home with him and spend the weekend at his place in the city. I said yes. He had paid so much attention to me in the days we had already spent together. He seemed genuinely interested in me, he seemed genuinely attracted to me, and I was swooning.

On Eric's home dresser was the photo of him with Ram Dass that he had emailed me when we first started seeing each other. He told me the photo had been taken by a previous girlfriend. She was one of several women he described as crazy "shark women," who he claimed wanted to date him because of his powerful position. He mentioned his ex-wife, who continued to serve as his advisor; he referred to her as a "stone-cold killer." He said he had never met anyone like me. He made me feel different and also separate from the women before me. He made me not want to know who they were.

He looked at the scars on my body and with sympathetic eyes told me he admired my ability to deal with adversity. (In May 2012, I had surgery to remove two cancers, thymoma and a gastrointestinal stromal tumor [GIST].) I said that there were many people who had dealt with far more adversity than I would ever know.

"You're a good turnip," he said in a sincere and complimenting tone. He had already come up with an affectionate nickname for me, based on the title of my website, "Tanya Turns Up." It was a nickname I had gotten in college because I was known for turning up at friends' events.

My scars had long been a source of insecurity for me. On the one hand, I thought they were very punk rock, thin, jagged lines that separated the left and right sides of my body. On the other hand, they were a visible marker of my having been sick. A scar runs down the length of my torso in three parts. It starts above my heart and pauses near the center of my rib cage. There is a small mark where a chest tube was. The scar resumes below my navel and ends at the top of my pelvic bone.

In fall 2012, just a few months after my surgery, my former husband told me he wanted to separate. We were in France, on tour with a show that he was directing and I had produced and was also in. His announcement came on the heels of a trying few years during which I had endured three miscarriages and an attempt at fertility treatment that was abruptly cut short when the tumors were discovered. Instead of making a new life, I had been obliged to save my own.

I had started writing *The Big Lie* while I was in the midst of pursuing fertility treatment. I was shaken up by how many friends and friends of friends had stories to tell, too, about their own experiences with infertility and their lack of in-depth fertility awareness. I had decided to aggregate what I was learning and speak to experts about what they wished people knew.

By the time I turned in the manuscript, my life had taken so many twists and turns, with the surgery to remove the tumors and the problems in my marriage, that even my editor was surprised by what he read.

When I wasn't working on the book, I was on my knees with grief, mourning the loss of a life I had thought would last the rest of my days. I thought maybe it would come back. My former husband was not making any moves to pursue divorce; he made it seem as if he were going through stuff and needed to figure things out. But a year later, at my book release party, a woman who had worked with both of us revealed that my husband had actually been in a relationship with another woman who had also worked with us—his assistant director, whom many friends had warned me about. They thought she was angling to take my place. One had said, "She wants your life." But I dismissed their concerns. I never felt jealous. Also, I would tell them, "She's a lesbian." Which she was, and in a relationship with another woman.

I think it was the day after my book party, or soon thereafter, that I contacted a lawyer and pushed forward with getting a divorce. I felt that he had moved on, and so I needed to as well. I never thought my husband was a bad person. He had just done a bad thing. At times, I felt he could have killed me with the brutality and timing of his actions. But there was something liberating about knowing the truth. I focused on my recovery and not feeling any bitterness.

That was the beginning of the next phase of my life. I started spending more time in Portland, Oregon, where my best friend from college lived, and I would visit him there at least once a year. It's my happy place, where my shoulders instantly relax as soon as I land at the airport.

It took me a while after my divorce to feel that I could even look at a man in a sexual way. I felt nervous when there was even just an inkling of attraction. I had scars on my torso that hadn't been there before I met my former husband. I thought they might unnerve men if I took my clothes off; I thought my body looked like that of a sick person. Also, my husband had said he wanted to separate after, not before, I had the scars.

One of the more hurtful things my ex said to justify his leaving was that he had been going along with the relationship, that what we had been were great business partners (though, he added, "passionate ones"). In that moment, I thought, "Wow, everything I thought was real was not." I felt like I had been completely duped by someone who had been using me in many ways. But as time went by, I thought, "Well, he's just another Mr. Transactional."

By the time I met Eric, I felt like I was ready to be with someone again. His values seemed aligned with mine. He was worshipped by those around him. He seemed like he would be a good boyfriend. At the time, he seemed like the opposite of my ex-husband. What primarily attracted me to Eric was that he made overt statements about being transformational rather than transactional.

The week after spending that first weekend at his place, I

went to New Haven, Connecticut, to work with Carrie Mae Weems on her show at the Yale Repertory Theatre. While I was there, Eric called often, so often that Carrie remarked that he already seemed like he couldn't be without me. He also sent me songs via email: "The Way You Look Tonight" and "You'd Be So Nice to Come Home To."

What an unexpected turn of events in my life. I had thought that eventually I would meet someone, but I didn't foresee that that person would be the attorney general of New York State, a political rising star, and a very powerful man.

CHAPTER 2

ENTRAP

On his desk at home was a copy of *Dark Money*, by Jane Mayer. On the bookshelf in his office at 120 Broadway was a copy of *Life on the Outside*, by Jennifer Gonnerman, a longtime friend of mine. I took these as good omens.

I attended a talk Eric was giving with two meditation teachers. The theme was the relationship between spirituality and social engagement, how to stay aligned during the turbulent times before the election. The teachers were part of Eric's group of friends involved with activism and spirituality. They would check in with each other periodically by sending an email to confirm that they had paused to meditate and take in their surroundings.

Looking back, I see how I got sucked in. His outward-facing spirituality was a mask for the torment beneath the surface. His outward-facing feminism was a mask for his misogyny. Through public events like the one that night, he perpetuated a narrative of himself as an agent of change and transformation. Many people I trusted depicted him as a hero, and he positioned himself as standing up for many causes I believed in. So I bought it.

In between college and law school, he had worked at a clinic that provided abortions, and he gave women rides from the airport to the clinic and comforted them. He had been a deputy sheriff in the Berkshires and befriended prisoners there. He showed me a letter that an inmate had written him, thanking him for his kindness. He frequently told a story about how the New York state GOP had tried to cut him out of the state senate by reshaping his district to be mostly Dominican, knowing he didn't speak Spanish. So he had taught himself Spanish, pounded the pavement within the newly drawn lines, and won. He introduced me to many of his allies in the Latinx community. When I went with him to have dinner with a Dominican American congressperson, Eric seemed proud to show me off. I went from feeling like I was not the typical politician's girlfriend to feeling like my being brown was an asset to his ambitions; he often talked about running for governor one day.

He made a concerted effort to support me in my world. He came to an Artists for Hillary gathering in Brooklyn that I had helped put together, and he spoke to the group. He came to pick me up from the campaign headquarters after I had a meeting there. But I also realized that my world, which at the time included collaborating with many Clinton staffers, provided him with a personal connection to the campaign. It was something I could add to his profile. If only I could have seen how horribly wrong everything would go, politically and personally—the negativity and chaos in one sphere influenced the other.

But it wouldn't be fair to assert that our relationship was only about what I could do for him. It also made sense in the context of the work we both were engaged in. And perhaps most important, there was tenderness and camaraderie between us. There was communication. I felt that he wanted to be a good boyfriend.

Many of my friends thought he was a catch. They also thought I was in for a wild ride, with a front-row seat to the national political theater. Suddenly, I was becoming a repository for behind-the-scenes details.

Attending high-profile events was not new to me; as a producer and artist, I went to my share of galas and openings. But when I attended with Eric, I was "the girlfriend." I felt elevated in terms of clout but diminished in terms of my achievements in my own right.

Soon after we began dating, he took me to the Global Citizen Festival in Central Park, where we were escorted onstage and stood in the wings. Metallica was playing. I was amused that Eric didn't know who they were. That same month, he took me to the wedding of a congressman's son. We were seated with a politician I happened to know. He was surprised that I was with Eric. He said something to the effect that it was good for Eric, but maybe not for me. He said it in a joking way; in retrospect, I wondered if there was something behind that comment.

Eric and I were becoming more enmeshed. I was now his regular companion at intimate dinners with politicians and important donors and at outings to Jazz at Lincoln Center, his favorite venue. These were amazing times: going to Dizzy's Club to hear Joey Alexander, the young Indonesian jazz piano prodigy; going backstage to say hi to Wynton Marsalis; attending each other's events and cheering each other on; talking openly and honestly about our hopes and fears; dancing around his apartment.

But other patterns were emerging. He was often asking me for connections, for fundraising, for volunteers. I didn't think much of these requests at the time; a lot of people asked me for favors. But he seemed to be interested in my friends only if they could be of some use to him. When we had dinner with friends of mine, our relationships in some cases dating back to college, he would seem uninterested in hearing about their lives. He seemed to want to talk only about himself and what he was doing as attorney general. After some of these dinners, he would refer to my friends as "ditzes" or "clueless"—but these were successful, Harvard-educated women.

Politicians have to be charismatic so that when they say "Jump," people ask "How high?" Abusers are often charismatic, too. Politicians and abusers can share another characteristic: extreme narcissism. When I later read Beverly Engel's book *The Emotionally Abusive Relationship,* I understood more how narcissistic personality disorder (NPD) leads to abusive behavior. Engel writes, "Those with NPD are often oblivious to others and how their behavior affects them." She also explains that "too much closeness terrifies the narcissistic individual and so he criticizes or imposes control on his partner to hold her at bay."

At first, Eric was so adoring and supportive of me that I didn't take note of his extreme narcissism, such as when he emailed me article after article about himself. Also, if the outcome of the election was going to be as all the pundits predicted, Eric would be more prominent than ever, and I would be by his side. I was feeling an adrenaline rush from the romance and headiness of my new relationship.

CHAPTER 3

ISOLATE

On Election Day, November 8, 2016, I rolled out of bed and voted. At the time, I was still on social media. I scrolled through photo after photo of people excited that America might finally have a female president after nearly a century of women having the right to vote. Women posted photos of themselves holding their daughters with the caption "I VOTED FOR HER." I myself posted a photo in which I held a Hillary sign.

Prior to that day, I had already begun talking with staffers on the campaign about ideas for the inauguration. I had proposed having women heads of state from around the world record congratulatory messages for Hillary, acknowledging her historic moment. Eric was similarly brimming with confidence about the outcome.

He and I had a full night of viewing parties and celebrations to attend. I put on a new, bright-pink knee-length cape dress and heels. I preferred to wear boots, flats, or sneakers, but Eric always wanted me in heels at events. I had gotten my hair done because he always wanted me to wear my hair up or blown straight. Otherwise, he often said my hair looked wild.

First, we went to a party hosted by Harvey Weinstein at Cipriani Downtown, but we left after a short time to get to our next stop. By the time we got there, the tide was already turning for the worse, and a somber cloud was descending. We didn't stay long and soon made our way to the Javits Center, where it felt like everyone was on a sinking ship. We were taken to a VIP area, where many celebrities seemed to be in tears. The main hall was teeming with people in a state of paralysis, their disbelieving eyes glued to monitors. A journalist friend who was covering the election told me over the phone that it was over, based on the results that were coming in. An outdated Electoral College, voter suppression and manipulation, and false information spread by Facebook were going to result in the bad guys winning. We had only been pretending that we lived in a democracy.

A day that had started with boundless promise was ending in utter devastation, not just for me but for the majority of Americans. The existential threat that Donald Trump's candidacy posed to the country was coming to pass. The misogyny and racism he embodied would be unleashed.

A little before midnight, Eric and I went home, though the election had not yet been called. We each received call after call from friends and colleagues who wanted to be comforted. I felt that whatever the outcome, now our real work had to begin.

The next morning, when I emerged from his apartment, a gray pall seemed to hang over the city streets. Most people looked gray, too, as if the life force were being sucked out of them. We lived in the city that had built Trump, a city that had allowed him to cannibalize it for his personal profit. We were confronted by his name on buildings throughout the city.

Here was a man who at every opportunity had stoked the worst impulses of humankind. Take, for example, his behavior during the Central Park Jogger case, a violent rape that tore the city apart in 1989. The following year, five innocent black and brown boys were wrongly convicted of the crime, and Trump played an outsized part in convincing the public that they were guilty. He appeared on television news and took out full-page newspaper ads calling for the death penalty. Eventually, the five boys were exonerated, but by then their lives had been destroyed and degraded. Trump, predictably, has never apologized or shown remorse.

I happened to have friends who knew people who had been entangled with him and had had disturbing experiences, such as a woman he dated who supposedly was forbidden to touch his hair or use his bathroom, and who was told to avoid being photographed with him because she was a woman of color. One friend told me a story about his close friend who had lived in a building that Trump bought. Attempting to force the tenants to leave, Trump deployed ruthless tactics with the help of a new management agency, which cut off the heat and hot water and let garbage pile up to attract rodents. Tales of Trump's nefarious and insidious behavior throughout his life and career were well known in New York circles.

Because of his previous legal battles with Trump, Eric was now in a position to defend New York against the Trump administration. He spent the day after the election consoling his staff and strategizing for the future. He started rallying Democratic attorneys general around the country to prepare for the attacks on civil liberties and vulnerable communities that were sure to come. Meanwhile, because of the work I had done during the election, I was approached by friends and acquaintances about what to do next. I felt at a loss. I had really hoped that after the election, I would be able to sail off into the sunset and get back to focusing on art and social justice causes. I thought that my work with American politics would be done. But for the moment, I had to continue. Also, I was now a politician's girlfriend, and I threw myself into the role.

I did what I could to give people ideas for how to keep going. I started a newsletter that highlighted how people could get involved and offered words of inspiration. I come from Sri Lanka, which endured a brutal civil war for decades and had its own version of Trump—an autocrat who installed various family members in government and turned Sri Lanka into one of the most dangerous countries for journalists. I was sorry that America was about to experience a period of great tumult, but it wouldn't be the first such period, and I felt America would come out on the other side.

Around the holidays, Eric came with me to Sri Lanka to visit my family—which greatly impressed my relatives, that such an important person would make the exhausting journey to the other end of the world. While there, he was the most relaxed I had ever seen him. Even though the election had gone terribly wrong just a month before, he was now in a country that was very far away. He talked about how everything looked and smelled different. We would go for walks at the Galle Fort by the Indian Ocean. I took him scuba diving, and he said it was the best dive he had ever done. On Christmas Day, he helped my grandmother, with her two deteriorated hips, walk up the stairs of her home. He sat and talked with her.

But the darkness was starting to seep in; his need to isolate me from my family and friends was increasing. One day at my grandmother's house, where all my family were assembled, he turned to me suddenly and said, "I can't take much more of this."

I took it to mean he didn't want to be around my family anymore. I told him I had come all this way to see them, but he could do his own thing. The next day, he stayed at the hotel while I went to family gatherings.

Before we left Sri Lanka, my aunt organized an elaborate dinner for us. She made sure to have enough vegetables and fish because I told her Eric didn't eat meat. My family does eat meat, though, and there was a chicken dish. I am not a vegetarian, but he wouldn't allow me to eat meat in his presence. He saw me looking at the dish and glanced at me disapprovingly.

After we returned to America, I felt another series of dark pivots in our relationship. By this point, I was essentially living with him. I had gradually brought more and more of my belongings from my apartment to his place. We talked about possibly staying at my place some nights, spending a weekend downtown, but he said it would take too much coordination because of his need for security. I told him that my building had twenty-four-hour security guards and he could have his own security detail outside. But that didn't make a difference. We never stayed at my place.

I missed my life downtown, the ease of contact with my support network of friends and collaborators, but he didn't want me out of his sight. On one occasion, I was at a film event in Tribeca. It was pouring rain, and I was near my place. I left him a message that I was sorry, but I was going to stay downtown.

When I was a few blocks away from my house, he phoned, shouting at me, "I can't trust you!" A friend was walking beside me and looked alarmed. She could hear his angry tone through the phone.

Another time, I was receiving an award from a vocational training program for women of color. As the event ended, Eric called to say that he had landed unexpectedly early from Albany and needed dinner. He didn't ask me how the event had gone. He didn't congratulate me. He wanted me to leave right away and pick up food for him.

Later, my friend who had come with me to the event would say that she could hear his tone through the phone, and it freaked her out. She thought about him, "How dare he? She's not his slave. I don't care who he is." She was so troubled that she went home and told her husband but decided not to say anything to me.

Meanwhile, I was ignoring the signs. I felt that I was the one making mistakes.

One day, I went with a friend to see a Broadway show. She's like my sister, someone I can tell anything to. She asked how Eric was doing, and I said something to the effect of "There's a lot going on." She said, "You seem subdued in the relationship." Later, when I confided in her, she would say she wished she had asked more questions and read between the lines.

One night, Eric and I had dinner with a friend of mine from college and her husband. Later, my friend told me that she noticed how possessive he was of me; she noticed how much he drank; she noticed his narcissism; and although she thought he clearly loved me, she said it felt more like a validation of him. Another friend, when she met him, said she noticed how willing he was to objectify me into his life, how the focus was always on him. He didn't talk about me at all and seemed interested in my life only as it served him.

After the election, his drinking had started to acquire an increasingly dark undertone. As he became more comfortable with me, the addictions started to spill out; having me close to him was both a mirror and a crutch. I would wake up to find that he had eaten my yogurt directly from the container because he was hungry in the middle of the night after taking Ambien and lorazepam along with alcohol. Sometimes I would wake up to find him staggering around the apartment, and I would guide him back to bed.

When he was sober, I would sometimes describe to him his behavior during the night. His face would show regret and distress. I felt sorry for him because his pain was so deep that he was trying to annihilate himself. But I started to realize that he was trying to annihilate me, too. There was a growing dissonance between the man who cared deeply about me and the world and the dark man who wanted to obliterate himself and take me down with him.

He manipulated me by giving me things and then taking them away. Because he wanted me in his space, he offered me the guest room to use as my own. But he wouldn't let me put a desk in it so that I'd have a study. I had to work on the living room couch or at the dining table, but then he got annoyed that I was working in those areas. Eventually he said I could use his office, which he never used himself. However, the Wi-Fi didn't work there because the room was on the other side of the kitchen, far from the router. I couldn't do my work without the Internet. I felt like I couldn't move without committing an offense.

He wouldn't let me put a second closet in the guest room, so my clothes were squeezed into a small space until eventually he let me hang some things in his closet. I used the bathroom in the guest room, and when I would hand wash clothes there and hang them to dry, he said with annoyance that it looked like Chinatown. He kept confining me to narrower spaces while accusing me of taking up too much space.

Meanwhile, he was constantly asking me to listen to him practice his speeches and to work with his staff on inviting people to his fundraisers. He never showed gratitude and sometimes belittled how much I helped him, even though he seemed dependent on me. He would also accuse me of not creating enough separation between his work and our relationship, even when he was the one asking for my help.

But then there were times when he was present and positive. He talked about our moving into a bigger apartment so that I could have my own proper room to work in. He talked about our having children. That made me laugh. I would say, "Do you have any idea what my book is about?" *The Big Lie* was about my not being able to have children.

In January 2017, two nights before the presidential inauguration, I stayed at my place because I was supposed to speak at an event downtown the next day. Those rare nights in my own apartment were my best opportunities to get a good night's sleep. But the next morning, I got a call from him. He was in an emergency room. He told me he had drunk too much the night before and fallen in the bathroom. When he woke up, he was lying in a pool of blood. His security detail had taken him to the hospital. I asked if he wanted me to come. He said yes. On the way to the hospital, I called the person who had organized my talk and told her I was sorry, but I had to cancel.

When I arrived at the hospital, I saw how badly he had been bruised. He had a black eye and stitches around his eyebrow. He was supposed to do a press conference later that day. I told him he couldn't; his injury was too obvious and would elicit questions. He asked me to take a photo and send it to his communications person, which I did.

We went back to his apartment, where I tried my best to clean up the bloodstains that were all over the bedroom. In addition to his communications person, he talked with his ex-wife, a communications and political strategist with whom he still regularly consulted. After speaking with them, he said I was to tell anyone who asked that he had fallen while jogging—a curious explanation, since he rarely jogged.

What goes on in the house, I had learned, stays in the house. The cone of silence was closing in. If I betrayed it, I would be jeopardizing not only his career but also the service that he was doing for the country. How would it look if the attorney general of New York had gotten so drunk right before the inauguration that he ended up in the hospital?

He had already been making me feel trapped at home. Now he was gradually isolating me from the world outside. It wasn't just his substance abuse that I was made to feel I had to hide; I was also being more frequently exposed to encounters that shouldn't have happened in my presence. I felt he was being careless, having work conversations I shouldn't overhear. On some occasions, he said if we broke up he would have to kill me. I tried not to take him seriously, but I filed the remark away in my mind.

Numerous times, when we were together in public, people approached him as if he were the Second Coming. They would say "Save us." Occasionally, people in government or with close ties to government officials would call him or meet with him, offering what they claimed was inside intelligence on the current administration. They thought he was their best shot at delivering America from the clutches of a dangerous president. Even the president himself sent an envoy, one of his personal lawyers, to deliver a message to Eric: that he was sorry for the clashes they'd had in the past and hopeful that they could find common ground. He also wanted Eric to know that he was not really a Republican.

That's how powerful Eric was perceived to be.

I would think to myself, "If only they knew what a mess Eric is at home. If only they knew what he does to me."

The exchanges I witnessed added to my increasing disaffection with politics. Everyone, I was coming to see, was in collusion with everyone; no one was what they pretended to be. It was all about power and who got to wield it, and they didn't care about the people at all.

I was caught in a confusing system, and I was made to feel I couldn't talk to anyone about it.

CHAPTER 4

CONTROL

Often, when he looked at my chest, Eric would tell me to see his plastic surgeon and get rid of my scars. In the early days of our relationship, he spoke about my scars as if they were a badge of courage. But now, he would also tell me to get a boob job and to get in shape. He made me think, "If I want to be the First Lady, I have to change how I look."

When I described these interactions to a friend, she told me about her experience dating a future senator and presidential candidate while they were in college. When he broke up with her, he said, "You're not First Lady material." Clearly, for men with political ambitions, the way their partner looks impacts their prospects. In my situation, Eric's controlling of my appearance was a thread in a larger web of manipulation.

As his interest in meditation and Buddhism had grown, so had his interest in reconnecting with the faith of his birth: Judaism. He attended a synagogue in his neighborhood and started taking me with him. He told me stories about how Jared Kushner and Ivanka Trump had, years before, tried to befriend him. After all, he was the attorney general of New

York; he had jurisdiction over their families' businesses. When the three of them got together, they bonded over their commitment to Judaism. Ivanka, Eric said, was especially well versed in the teachings of the faith.

Jared and Ivanka would eventually become enemies of Eric's, especially after he brought the fraud case against Trump University. At the time, Jared was the publisher of the *New York Observer* and printed a front-page story about Eric with an illustration depicting him as the sinister Malcolm McDowell character from the film *A Clockwork Orange*.

I consider myself agnostic leaning toward atheist, but I didn't mind going with Eric to synagogue. I've attended places of worship of many denominations and recognize that congregating with others in a religious community provides people with comfort and purpose. One night, Eric asked me if I would consider converting. He said he would even take the classes with me. He wanted to draw me closer into his orbit.

However, he seemed uncomfortable when he was in mine. On my birthday, I was giving a talk about women's activism. Many friends attended. He came, too, which I thought was a wonderful gesture because he was so busy with his own events. Toward the end of the evening, my friends gathered around and a cake was brought out. But soon afterward, he insisted we leave immediately. My friends couldn't believe that he was making me leave my own birthday celebration. One later told me that his behavior was "jarring."

His forcing me to leave my own events happened on a number of occasions, including at a fundraiser I organized for him. A friend stood patiently by my side, waiting to meet him after he had finished talking with another guest, but he suddenly said we had to leave. I told him I wanted him to meet my friend. He gave me an agitated look and hurried me toward the door. My friend tried to walk with us, to have at least a few words with him.

She said, "I want to know who this person is who has won my friend's heart."

But he couldn't have cared less. He looked at her blankly, opened the door to the car, and motioned for me to get in. Afterward, she told another friend, "I don't like him. Tanya can't be herself around him."

He didn't like me talking on the phone, even though he was often on the phone himself. If he heard me on the phone in another room with the door closed, he would come, open the door, glare at me, and shake his head. I would try to wrap up the call quickly.

During one call with my mother, she said, "You get very quiet when he's around. My friends notice when I try to talk to you." His manipulation of me was like what Patricia Evans describes in her book *The Verbally Abusive Relationship*: "Control and dominance seem to give the abuser a sense of power, security, and identity as a male."

Eric's need to subjugate me extended to our sexual interactions. When he first slapped me in the face after we started making love, it happened in the blink of an eye. No man had ever done that to me. He seemed to be testing me. I didn't know what to do. I tried to make sense of it. Before that point, we had gotten to know each other over the course of about six weeks, and I thought of him as a meditator, someone who espoused spirituality and who fought on behalf of vulnerable people. At that moment, I became aware that he could inflict great harm on me.

Over time, the slaps got harder and began to be accompanied by demands. In bed, he would slap me until I agreed to find him a young girl for a three-way. I told him what he wanted to hear even though I knew it was never going to happen. He would slap me until I agreed to call him "Master" or "Daddy." He recounted his fantasies of finding me somewhere far away to be his slave, his "brown girl." He would hurl spit into my mouth and mash his lips against mine so that it was hard for me to breathe. A few times, he put his hands around my throat and tried to choke me. I would try to move his hands, but he would order me to put my hands down. I would say, "Hey, that hurts." I would tell him to stop. But he didn't respond to my protests. Each time, he looked at me as if he were possessed, and then the moment passed quickly. I felt as if I had vertigo. I was scared.

I didn't realize it at the time, but I was dealing with one kind of abuse that can go on between people in committed relationships: intimate violence. But I had convinced myself that he would be my partner, maybe for life. If I wanted to keep him, I felt I had to let him dominate me.

I tolerated the situation because it was disorienting and so disconnected from the person he presented as in public. By day, he was the crusading attorney general, and he had to be nimble and sober. At night, as soon as he got home, he would start swigging from a bottle, usually wine, but sometimes vodka. I tried to get him to pour it into a glass so he could keep track of how much he was consuming. He would pour me a glass of bourbon and push it toward me, saying, "Drink your bourbon, turnip."

But watching the way he drank at home made me not want to drink myself. He took the joy out of having a drink to wind down at the end of the night. He made me feel as if I had to be his caretaker in case he drank too much. He would take Ambien and lorazepam at the same time. I told him that the combination of these drugs and alcohol made people do crazy things.

Sometimes, I was woken up by the sound of him watching movies or television beside me in bed, with the volume up loud. He liked to watch *Sneaky Pete*, *The Americans*, and clips from late-night talk shows. I would say that I needed to rest and maybe I should sleep in the guest room, which would make him upset. Other times, I would be woken up by his fingers inside me or his hands squeezing parts of my body. He seemed to be moving in his sleep and would say things like "I love you" or "My bad, bad girl, Daddy's going to rape you." I remember on a few occasions, after he had passed out, going to the guest room and sitting down with tears falling down my cheeks.

He started asking me to hide the bottles from him. But in the morning, I would discover that he had found them, even if they had been in my bag of dirty laundry, and the bottles would be empty. He blamed me for not hiding them well enough.

I longed for signs of affection and intimacy. When we had those moments, I was happy with him, dancing around the apartment as he played me his favorite songs, lying in bed or on the couch in an embrace. I tolerated the times when we had sex and he slapped me and spat at me, calling me his property and his brown slave. I thought, "I can put up with that much." As long as the abuse wasn't happening the majority of the time—maybe one day out of a week—I was able to compartmentalize it. This was how I coped with the situation. But I began to piece together that I was in an endless cycle of abuse.

He made me feel that he needed me, and I felt empathy for him. His parents had had a bitter divorce, and because they didn't want anything to do with each other, they had neglected him. I could feel the loneliness that he had carried with him throughout his life as a result. Many times, he would look into my eyes and ask, "Are you going to take care of me?"

I wanted to love him completely. For a while, I did. I also bought into the notion of us: as he rose in his field, I thought, I would rise with him. He would say, "We're a good team." We could accomplish so much together. We could help change the world. But he was Dr. Jekyll and Mr. Hyde, and I never knew which would be dominant—especially at night, when he was drinking.

When things were bad, I dissociated. I thought the situation would calm down, that he would change. I thought the good side would win. But I had never seen someone I was in a relationship with so out of control and dependent on uppers and downers. A few times, he acknowledged that he needed help, but he was worried that if he got it, the world would find out. I was made to feel that there had to be a shroud of silence around the subject. But I encouraged him to at least talk to a therapist. I even had him speak on the phone with mine. After fifteen minutes, he ended the call and said he was fine.

In February, about a month after the incident around the inauguration that landed Eric in the hospital, I had lunch with a director friend, and we talked about how things were not going well. I told her that Eric was depressed and I was trying to help him. She had been with us at a dinner with some filmmakers who wanted to make a documentary about him. But in the weeks since they first approached him and his team about the idea, I had become concerned that Eric could be so un-self-aware as to think having cameras follow him around wouldn't be a disastrous idea. I told my friend that I didn't think Eric should be part of the documentary. Later, after the *New Yorker* story, she reached out to me and said she'd realized she could have read between the lines.

There were also times when *I* was the one not reading between the lines, when people tried to warn me. When I first started seeing Eric, a friend and mentor had tried to tell me over dinner, "I want you to be careful. I've heard—" The waiter arrived, and she didn't finish the thought after he left. A year later, as I started to write down for myself every bit of pain that I had experienced with him, I reached out to my friend and asked if she remembered what she had wanted to tell me. Without hesitation, she said, "Yes, I heard he has a reputation for using and abusing women, then discarding them."

Another friend told me, when I told her early on about his drinking, that she was worried. Later, when I told her that he slapped and spit at me almost every time we had sex, she was shocked but not surprised.

I had always wondered if he had done that to his previous girlfriends and sexual partners, but I also wondered if the abuse was specific to me. He told me he'd never been with anyone like me. He praised my activism and my work, yet he demeaned and humiliated me.

The darkness increasingly seeped into our daytime and nonsexual interactions through his criticisms and need to control me. On many occasions, I told him that I felt he was trying to ruin my self-esteem. He said he was depressed. The times were turbulent; he was going to work on himself. He prayed and meditated. I had seen him give presentations on meditation and its connection to his commitment as an advocate for vulnerable communities, including women. Sometimes we would meditate together, and in those moments, I felt hopeful and at ease with him. But spiritual practice increasingly was not enough to reconcile the conflict between what he said and what he did, between his daytime and late-night behavior.

I meditate every morning. It's a practice I began when I was sick. During those fifteen minutes, when my thoughts wander, I mine my memory for connections between my past and my present. I've made many mistakes, but I am essentially the woman I wanted to be: I went to graduate school. I'm an artist and producer. For my whole career, I have been working with organizations that stand up for the rights and safety of women and girls.

I grew up around domestic violence. In my earliest memory, I am clutching a stuffed white bunny as I stand in the living room, crying at the top of my lungs, watching my father—who towers over my mother by almost a foot—with his hands raised. I must have been three years old. I think at one point my father kicks my mother. They are cursing each other. He calls her a bitch; she calls him a shit. These fights happened only at night, as if both of them had alter egos that came out after dark. Their nighttime alter egos hated each other more passionately than they disliked each other during the day. My father, a psychiatrist, had encountered many split personalities—how was it, I sometimes wonder, that he never conquered his own? Yet at the same time, as a child, I watched *Superman*. I was Wonder Woman on many Halloweens, and my favorite doll was the Bionic Woman. It's human, I suppose, to want to be two people.

I am terrified by the memory of my father beating my mother. But I also remember how much I loved the stuffed bunny in my hand.

A few years later, after we moved from an apartment to a big house—a beautiful house, with rose bushes and a pool, and a view of a golf course that I would sneak onto—I rushed into my parents' bedroom in the middle of the night. I had heard screams; I had heard those now-familiar curse words. I was maybe eight years old. My father again towered above my mother, but this time I was tall, too. I grabbed his hands and held them tightly so he couldn't beat her.

As I got older, the beatings became less frequent, because I was there to witness them and restrain my father. One day, when he attempted to beat my mother, before I could intervene, she called the cops. But she had me to be her police, so I couldn't see what she could achieve by this except bringing shame, not just on my father but on all of us. Now we had an "incident" on record. The cops stood at the door of my bedroom, attempting to ask me questions, but I wondered what good it would do to answer. I was watching television—*Land of the Lost*, a series about a family that travels back in time to the age of the dinosaurs—and I was happy to be in another universe. I heard my mother say to them, "She doesn't want to get married because of what she sees with me."

Was that true? Was that what my mother believed?

These are not snapshots; they are black holes into which sinks the translucence of my existence. I used to avoid discussing these memories, not because they were painful but because I felt they tainted me. When I was young, I learned to put up a positive front and conceal the horrors I was dealing with at home. I kept my family's secrets. Perhaps my own experience with intimate partner violence is what has propelled me to write this and make more sense of my memories.

In Margaret Atwood's introduction to *The Handmaid's Tale*, she writes about "the Dear Reader for whom every writer writes." The act of writing is hopeful because it implies that there is a reader, the Dear Reader, out there. The Dear Reader is also the writer's future self; the writer can later refer to what has been written.

As I reveal my memories now, I know I am a child from an abusive household. How has that scarred me in ways I cannot see? My childhood made me stronger: As a teenager, I resolved to be happy. I resolved never to put up with abuse. I resolved never to enter into a marriage or a relationship that would trap me for eternity in the delusion that I belonged there. But yet, as I write this, I know that love above all else conquers hurt, conquers pain in life and of body. And I know I love my father. He was in all other roles—father, doctor, friend—a generous and compassionate man. I cannot reconcile his abuse of my mother with his good attributes, but I forgive him. Forgiveness is subjective.

When I saw my father hit my mother, I stood up to him. I looked up divorce lawyers in the phone book and made an appointment for my mother. Still, abuse happened to me. Yet what I experienced as an adult, in my forties, felt different from what I witnessed as a child. My father had given my mother a black eye, a bloody tooth. I remember her telling tales about her bruises: she fell, she hit her face on a door. I remember the inability of some people she confided in to believe that she was being abused. There are family and friends who to this day don't believe her or talk as if it was her fault.

Before Eric, I had never been in an abusive relationship. I had never been with an alcoholic. I had to figure out what to do. It took me a while to make the connection between my mother's experience with domestic violence and my own. Eric didn't hit me outside of the bedroom.

And I wasn't dealing with sexual harassment or assault in the workplace. My situation wasn't like that of the women who encountered Russell Simmons or Harvey Weinstein, who both had enablers that turned a blind eye until the entire world could see. I entered into it willingly; I walked through the door with Eric. I even felt sorry for him. I thought, "Poor him, he's so depressed, and he's dealing with so much. So many people are putting pressure on him to save the world."

Unlike some of the abusers unmasked by the Me Too movement, Eric was a serial monogamist. He didn't need to abuse dozens or hundreds of women to satisfy his hunger for power. He didn't need a different woman to abuse every day. For almost a year, he had me.

Once, during the day, out of nowhere, he said that he was getting bored because he didn't have anything like a three-way to look forward to. He would talk about friends of mine he found cute and suggest that maybe they'd be good candidates. At the time, the scandal around the divorce of Mel B of the

Spice Girls and her partner had recently broken; her ex had coerced her into having three-ways. I asked, "Do you really want to take that kind of risk?" I knew I wasn't going to have a three-way, like I knew I wasn't going to have my scars removed or get a boob job, but I was scared to tell him so. Instead, I tried to show him how trying a three-way would have negative consequences. I thought, "If I can't change how he thinks, maybe I can change how he behaves."

In Sally Field's memoir, *In Pieces*, she describes her relationship with the actor Burt Reynolds, which she said was "confusing and complicated, and not without loving and caring, but really complicated and hurtful to me." She writes, "By the time we met, the weight of his stardom had become a way for Burt to control everyone around him, and from the moment I walked through the door, it was a way to control me." When I read Field's words, I felt that she could have been describing my dynamic with Eric. I work hard every day to understand how I got into and stayed in a relationship that was so damaging to my soul. I heard the applause when Eric spoke, and I got swept up in it. Applause can be blinding.

CHAPTER 5

DEMEAN

I have sympathy for those who harm me. I always wonder what it is about their history that made them harmful; I want to understand them. But I also know that the older I get, the less I should tolerate when they treat me poorly and the more I should avoid them, because cumulatively their actions take a toll.

From the school to the street to the workplace, abuse is all around us. I think about the micro- and macroaggressions that most of us deal with in our lives, sometimes daily. I think about the insults I've had hurled at me from the time I was a child: the mean girl in elementary school who criticized my black lips, the ex-wife of my former boyfriend who referred to me as "that Paki," the old man on a London street who said, "Coolie bugger bastard, go home."

I think about toxic work environments. I have been fortunate to work mostly in welcoming situations, but twice I've put up with far more than I should have. The first time was in my twenties, when I started producing films. A fellow producer was constantly second-guessing and berating me. Others on the production tried to intervene, but he just couldn't help himself. After months and months of taking it and hoping it would go away, I finally said to him, "Fuck you"—which was not my style, but I had had enough and felt like I had to shut him up.

About fifteen years later, he spotted me in a restaurant and said a brief hello. Later he sent me this email:

> I never think of the days of making that movie with-
> out a twinge of guilt and shame, for being, well, not
> the best I would have liked to have been. I was a very
> unhappy person, and I just want to apologize, very
> belatedly, for being a less than pleasant partner, which
> I fear I was.

The second time I dealt with hostility in the workplace I was in my forties. I was in a job producing live events for an arts center, where I should have been able to thrive, and in many ways I did. But one person—sadly, a woman—had it in for me from the moment I walked through the door. Like the producer when I was in my twenties, she couldn't seem to help herself. She routinely dismissed my ideas, criticized me, and took an unconscionable amount of time to respond to me about simple matters. She also sought out every opportunity to make me feel that I didn't belong, making sure I wasn't invited to internal events. (Others at the organization, however, would invite me, and I enjoyed watching her glare as I entered the room.)

While I was dealing with this situation, a friend who had been in a similarly hostile work environment sent me an article by Eileen Hoenigman Meyer, a blogger who often writes about company culture: "If you find yourself working alongside that colleague who routinely undercuts you in meetings, puts you down in conversations or criticizes your work in front of others, take note. Those are telltale signs that he or she may be threatened by you. It's difficult to exhibit your professional best, while also trying to deflect the shade that your colleague is throwing your way." I sent the article to the human resources director at my job because it so perfectly captured what I had been enduring with my colleague. A few other women at the organization had reached out to me simply to have lunch but ended up confiding in me how they felt bullied by the same woman who had abused me. They were much younger and didn't tell human resources about their situations because they worried about their reputations and future career opportunities.

Sometimes women are worse to other women because they think there's not enough space for another woman to shine. But I believe in making space. There is enough room. Still, when someone's threatened by you, there's little you can do. I chose to focus on the work. If I had been younger, less experienced, with fewer opportunities, I might have been traumatized. Instead, I made a conscious decision to continue, because I believed in the higher mission of the project. I stuck it out, because in every other way the job was perfect for me, and everyone else was wonderful. But I vowed never to put up with such treatment again.

With Eric, I sometimes felt like he was trying to crush me, if not kill me, with his demeaning behavior. In *Coercive Control: How Men Entrap Women in Personal Life*, Evan Stark writes, "To make contemporary women their personal property, the modern man must effectively stand against the tide of history, degrading women into a position of subservience that the progress of civilization has made obsolete." In fact, with Eric, more stinging than his slaps was his verbal abuse: that he insisted on calling me his property and his slave during sex, that he criticized my scars and wanted me to get them removed by a plastic surgeon. I was disgusted that he wanted me to call him "Daddy" and referred to me as his daughter when he himself had a daughter. That was why when he gave me a choice to call him "Master" or "Daddy," I picked "Master." But that resulted in more of the slave fantasies he inflicted on me.

His attacks on my scars were symbolic of everything horrible he did to me—what Beverly Engels would define as emotional abuse, "any nonphysical behavior [or attitude] that is designed to control, intimidate, subjugate, demean, punish, or isolate another person through the use of degradation, humiliation, or fear." When I wore V-necks, he would look at my scar and tell me to get rid of it.

While on a plane, I saw in the shopping guide a T-shirt that read, "Scars are like tattoos but with better stories." I wear my scars as reminders of what I have been through. They mark me and, in a way, comfort me. Sometimes, scars are not visible. Sometimes, they come in the form of stories.

When the New Yorker story came out, many people doubted that somebody like me could have let such abuse happen. But I have weaknesses. Eric figured out what they were and seized on them. He once said, "Sometimes I look at you, and I'm like, Wow. Sometimes I'm not sure." A comment like this, in isolation, is a jerky thing to say. It indicates he's kind of an asshole.

But taken in the context of the totality of Eric's behavior and actions, it became part of a pattern to demean me and make me feel less than. As Patricia Evans writes, "Verbal abuse is secretive . . . [It] becomes more intense over time. The partner becomes used to and adapted to it . . . Verbal abuse consistently discounts the partner's perception of the abuse."

For Thanksgiving 2016, Eric wanted to host a "Jew-Bu" celebration at his home for a small group of friends who were part of his meditation circle. Although I offered to cook, he wanted to have the event catered, but he asked me to make a curry to add to the meal. I spent hours buying the ingredients and preparing the dish, but before everyone arrived, he tasted what I had made and said it wasn't good. He didn't want to serve it. I was incredibly hurt. I also thought that was bullshit; I had been cooking since I was a child, first for my parents and then in various restaurants. In high school, I worked at a place called Raspberries in Andover, Massachusetts, which would offer "Tanya's Tuesday Special." I liked to make Thai or Indian dishes. In college, I was a cook at one of the first fine-dining restaurants that catered to a gay clientele in Boston. It was called Club Café, and my friend Thomas played the piano in the lounge. As an adult, I hosted dinner parties at which I made elaborate multicourse meals. But my cooking wasn't good enough for Eric to serve to his friends. My curry went unserved and was thrown away.

This analysis by Pamela Evans would later resonate with me: "Verbal abuse is, in a sense, built into our culture. One-upmanship, defeating, putting down, topping, countering, manipulating, criticizing, hard selling, and intimidating are accepted as fair games by many. When these power plays are enacted in a relationship and denied by the perpetrator, confusion results." I felt like I had failed Eric with my cooking, and perhaps that was his intention. As long as he could make me doubt myself, gaslight me, he could control me.

Writing this book sank me into a profound depression. Although it has ultimately been a catharsis, reviewing all the notes I had taken in real time brought back the experience of being with someone who made me feel extremely bad about myself. It also triggered memories of how I had felt belittled by important people in my life since I was a child. My mother often criticized me; I frequently felt like I couldn't move without committing a transgression. That feeling of entrapment is one I continue to struggle with.

I do not have good memories of childhood. The friction between my parents made for an unhappy home. I really do believe my parents tried their best with regard to how they treated me, but they took out on me their frustrations with each other. My father tried to make me feel sorry for him. My mother tried to control me.

I wet the bed a lot as a child. I also sometimes wet myself when awake. I remember standing in my kindergarten class as my mother came to pick me up after a Christmas pageant. She was standing in the doorway and could tell I needed to go to the bathroom. She was nudging me with her eyes to make haste and come to her, but I was frozen in my tracks. As the warm urine streamed down my legs, I felt like I was in a dark tunnel. I heard the teacher say, "Oh, someone has had an accident."

My mother grabbed my hand and took me away. She was embarrassed and angry; I was sad and ashamed. When those moments of wetting myself happened, I felt terribly lacking in agency over my body. As a teenager, I became bulimic. My mother said my father blamed her for my bulimia. Do I blame my mother? Yes and no. Yes because she didn't allow me the space within our family to have positive self-esteem. No because I was actually hazed into throwing up by two cruel girls at my boarding school. They brought me into the dorm bathroom and instructed me to drink a lot of water and then stick my fingers down my throat. I wonder if I would have become bulimic if I hadn't encountered those girls. It's not something I would have figured out how to do myself.

I also didn't blame my mother because she was similar to many mothers, especially the stereotype of the Asian mother: rather than praise her daughter, the Asian mother tends to demean her. I've heard the writer-director Lulu Wang talk about her mother's blasé reaction to Wang's success with her movie *The Farewell*. Wang said that it wasn't because her mother was mean but because she subscribed to the mind-set that "the higher you climb, the more I'm afraid you're going to fall."

There are many reasons that I was susceptible to developing an eating disorder: being criticized by my mother about my dress, weight, and looks; often feeling bad about myself; my disaffection from a world in which a civil war was raging in my birth country. I didn't want to die, but I wanted to disappear. I felt a tension between my exterior and my gut. Also, I was taking the torment I harbored inside because of the violence between my parents and exorcising it through vomiting. I am heartbroken now thinking about my behavior back then. It was as if I dissociated myself as an intellectually successful and even popular student from the privately self-destructive girl I also was.

In elementary school, I was bullied at times. Black girls

picked on me, and white girls picked on me, too. There was the mean girl, named Molly, who taunted me about my "black lips"; other kids called me "Tonto" or "Pocahontas." They didn't know the difference between an Indian and a Native American, or between an Indian and a Sri Lankan. I went along with it. I kept quiet. That's what I usually did: I kept quiet. Even as an adult, I was called "Pocahontas" in a derogatory way. I remember twice in one week in the 1990s, during my early days in New York, men on the street catcalling me: "Pocahontas, come here."

In high school, I was the rare girl taking quantum mechanics and vector calculus at the same time. I threw myself into my studies and focused on friends and teachers who helped me thrive. And I had a flair for the avant-garde. I got into acting; theater got me out of my shell, my skin.

At my college graduation, I won a theater award. After the ceremony, instead of congratulating me, my mother, who disapproved of my theatrical pursuits, said in a negative tone, "You've been acting." She also added, "You think people are going to hire you with your brown skin?"

I think her verbal abuse stemmed from her need to take out my father's abuse of her on me in some way. She was never made to feel good about herself by him, so she couldn't make me feel good about myself.

That moment after the Christmas pageant when I was four years old and wet myself in front of my whole class is one of my most vivid memories. To this day, I am prone to stage fright. I think I love theater in part because it helps me face my fears. Susan Cain, in her book *Quiet*, points out that public speaking is the number one fear in America. She writes, "Public speaking phobia has many causes, including early childhood setbacks, that have to do with our unique personal histories, not inborn temperament."

I was a shy child, made more so by the feeling I had secrets to hide about my life at home, because I was a witness to horrific domestic violence. After I read Cain's book, I felt that I was an introvert who had trained herself to be an extrovert just so I could participate in the world and stop having people talk about how shy I was. Once, when I was cleaning out boxes in my mother's home, I came across a stack of my old report cards. Comment after comment from various teachers echoed a similar sentiment: I was quiet. One teacher wrote, "Tanya seems shy out of almost excessive respect for everyone." But I was also the smartest girl in the class, and I would rather be smart than loud.

As strong and confident as I seem now, I have my weaknesses, and their roots go back to my childhood. As Beverly Engel writes, "The truth is, few people put up with emotional abuse as an adult unless they were abused as a child. And nearly every person who becomes emotionally abusive has a history of such abuse in childhood." She also argues that women tend to hold anger inside and become self-destructive, while men tend to inflict their anger on others.

Eric had told me about his painful childhood. When his parents divorced, they had such animus toward each other that they insisted on calling Eric by two different names; one parent called him by his first name, the other by his middle name. He was essentially always a bifurcated person. I thought it made sense that his favorite television shows, like *Sneaky Pete* and *The Americans*, were often about people who led double lives.

Toward the end of our relationship, when I was staying mostly at my own apartment, I had to go by his place to pick up my Mass General ID card; I was about to leave for my annual follow-up CT scan. When I walked in, I saw him with more open eyes. Now that I had distance and more objectivity, I saw less of the mask that had kept me with him. I asked how he was doing, meaning on an emotional level, and he prattled on about his poll numbers being down and his fundraising goals being off. He seemed hollow.

He said he was trying to be mindful of making me feel bad about myself. Then, a few minutes later, he asked if I was wearing perfume. I said yes. He said it was "strong," in a negative way. I had on the same perfume I always wore, the one he usually said he loved.

Intimate partner violence tends to happen in the shadows, behind closed doors, cloaked in secrecy. As Evan Stark explains, "Without an 'audience' for their victimization, the 8 to 10 million women experiencing coercive control in the United States remain in a twilight zone, disconnected and undocumented." As I reflect on how I got into an abusive relationship for the first time as a woman in her forties—one who, in the intervening years between childhood and middle age, became an independent person—I think that the little girl in me is still there, feeling bad about herself, and she needs to be set free. Writing it out like this, here, is part of that process.

CHAPTER 6

ABUSE

The pattern of abuse in my relationship with Eric was becoming clearer, but I was ensnared in the web that had been woven around me. Nonetheless, I was having a harder time reconciling my experience of him with the outside world's perception of him. He was not the man I thought he was. He was a hypocrite.

But why was I still there? Why was I still keeping it to myself? As I write these questions, I wonder if you, the reader, believe me. Do you believe that I was in an abusive relationship?

In *"Not to People Like Us": Hidden Abuse in Upscale Marriages*, Susan Weitzman explains "the dynamics that lie behind the intense secrecy surrounding the abuse." The victim feels a sense of isolation, and that isolation "is then fueled by the very real fear that no one will believe her and that she might be rejected if she speaks up—a fear that compounds both her silence and isolation." Victims also feel embarrassment and shame.

And yet a victim is one of millions. Weitzman writes:

When we think of love and marriage, we do not think
about domestic violence. Moonlight and roses are not
supposed to turn into beatings and threats upon one's
life. Yet, four million women nationwide are victims
of domestic violence per year. Every twelve seconds
a woman suffers this sort of abuse at the hands of a
husband or lover.

When I was first dealing with cancer, a doctor friend told
me that if you scanned anyone on the street, you'd probably
find something wrong with them. Following from that analogy,
I believe that if you scratched the surface of most people, you'd
probably find some history of abuse.

Why does anyone get caught up in an abusive relationship?
How fragile our minds can be when they are led by our hearts.
How lacking in agency we can be when we think we are in a
situation that will turn around if we stick with it.

After I shared my story, so many friends told me about
their own experiences. One friend wrote:

> I was in a relationship that was far more verbally
> abusive (and a bit financially abusive). He slapped
> me once, and I broke up with him. So, in some ways,
> the intimate partner violence was what liberated me.
> I wondered why I hadn't left earlier and began to
> question what my own role was—not in the sense
> of "blaming the victim," but every relationship is an
> ecosystem, and I no longer wanted to be part of any
> ecosystem like that! It led me deeper into therapy, etc.

In her case, she left as soon as the abuse became physical.
Another friend wrote about two horrific relationships:

> The first time I experienced violence in my seem-
> ingly well-matched relationship, it felt surreal, like I
> was watching my life through a tunnel. We had been
> together for a little over a year. While we shared a
> passionate, fun, exciting connection with many shared
> interests and dreams of the future, he was deep in the
> vortex of a drawn-out divorce and I was grieving the
> death of my father and a job transition happening at
> the same time. It was a tough time for both of us,
> but we were trying to take care of ourselves and each
> other. One night, after what seemed like a perfectly
> normal evening, we were lying quietly in bed and he
> asked: "Am I making you sad?" I answered, "Well, yes,
> the divorce process, your wife's anger and what it is
> doing to you and us is making me sad. So yes, I guess,
> yes." Suddenly, he flew into a rage and started scream-
> ing and hitting things and freaking out. He swung at
> the headboard of the bed, missing my head by a few
> inches. My blood ran cold, like ice. I threw him out of
> the apartment, stunned, shocked, overwhelmed, con-
> fused. He came back in the morning, remorseful, say-
> ing, "I am so ashamed." But he never said sorry. I gave
> him an ultimatum to seek help immediately, but he
> delayed. And then, three weeks later, he let his seven-
> year-old daughter hit me without reproach. I ended
> our relationship that day, and I haven't spoken to

him since. About a year later, in the aftermath of the previous breakup, I rekindled a relationship with a longtime lover. When I arrived at his home from the airport, he was acting a bit strange and distant (turns out he was using a variety of drugs that I didn't know about). I went to bed alone, a bit confused about his behavior since this wasn't how our reunions normally went. As I was resting in bed, half asleep, he stormed through the bedroom door and forced himself on me without speaking or consent. I didn't even seem to exist as a person in that moment. He was hurting me. Was he raping me? I remember thinking, "He doesn't see me as a human being. There is no one on this earth who cares about me." We broke up that week. Two years later, we met up again and I shared with him my experience of that night. He said he didn't remember. And he didn't apologize.

Our collective storytelling felt like a bloodletting. I saw more clearly how capable, independent women become ensnared. Even fierce women get abused.

Elizabeth Méndez Berry is a former journalist who wrote groundbreaking pieces about sexual harassment and relationship violence. Her 2010 article in *El Diario* titled "Street Harassment: The Uncomfortable Walk Home" highlighted the prevalence and damage of catcalling. "Though many catcallers don't have nefarious intentions, they don't put themselves in our shoes. Too often, it's a long, uncomfortable walk home." She continued: "But the problem is that a

'Good morning, beautiful' can instantly become 'Go to hell, bitch' if the gentleman in question doesn't take rejection well." In her reporting, she learned that "ten percent of women report quitting a job in order to avoid a harassment-heavy commute."

Méndez Berry also wrote several pieces about domestic violence in the music industry, one of which, "Love Hurts," won the ASCAP Foundation Deems Taylor/Virgil Thomson Award for music journalism. She told me, "Once you get to the point of physical abuse, there's usually so much emotional scaffolding that breaks you down. At the point that he hits you for the first time, he's often built up to that with lots of corrosive behavior."

In my relationship, I knew that I was being increasingly mentally and physically tormented. We couldn't have sex without him beating me, trying to strangle me, or insisting I call him "Master" or "Daddy" and submit to serving as his property. I want to be clear that I think it would be a terrible direction to police people's private lives. Desire is subjective; what's scary for one person could be kinky for another. But in my case, all this wasn't consensual; it wasn't exciting; it wasn't S&M; it wasn't sexual playacting. This was abusive, demeaning, threatening behavior. I felt like Offred in *The Handmaid's Tale*, who described sex with the Commander in this way: "What's going on in this room . . . is not exciting. It has nothing to do with passion or love or romance or any of those other notions we used to titillate ourselves with. It has nothing to do with sexual desire, at least for me . . . Arousal and orgasm are no longer thought necessary . . ."

Eric was taking out on me his need for power and his anxiety. It happened at night, in the dark, when I was naked, when it was more difficult to make an assertive decision. It happened when we were most intimate and I was most vulnerable, sometimes half-asleep in bed. Each time I expressed that I was in pain or asked him to stop, I was ignored and belittled. It felt like a bad dream.

In the morning, I would wake up, and another day would begin when I would see his good side, and I would be hopeful. Also, we didn't have sex every day. He told me he was old and not capable of frequent sex. The less I had sex with him, the more I could avoid his abuse in the bedroom. Many times, I deliberately tried to go to bed early.

As time went on, the slaps during sex got harder, and the belittling and demeaning of me carried over into our nonsexual encounters. The emotional and verbal abuse could now happen at any time, and as it started increasing, I began to feel like I was in hell. But he was also charming and charismatic, often supportive. I was constantly being pushed away from and pulled toward him.

I have tried to understand why I was susceptible. I thought I was mentally and emotionally stronger than him; I didn't realize that he was breaking me down through cumulative abuse. My former husband had left me when I was down, and I believe I was in an emotionally delicate state after the dissolution of my marriage. Also, the verbal abuse I had experienced from my mother, and the physical abuse she had experienced from my father and that I witnessed, made me more vulnerable to abuse myself.

In *Conflict Is Not Abuse*, Sarah Schulman writes:

Family based violence, sexual abuse, and its threat
surely have an influence on the ways that many
women understand their intimate relationships as
adults ... Growing up with chaos may make it harder
to know how to create order as an adult. We may be
more likely to make things worse, or initiate and
escalate conflict as adults if that was the model with
which we were raised.

When I saw my father hit my mother, it was in our living room, in our kitchen, not in their bed. As a result, I dissociated what I was experiencing with Eric from what I witnessed as a child. If he had hit me in the living room or kitchen, I think I would have been out of there almost immediately. I had always thought of myself as someone who would say, "The moment a man hits you, walk away. Walk away and don't come back unless he says he is getting professional help."

But the kind of violence I experienced during sex with Eric was hard to talk about. Also, I was more afraid to leave him than to stay with him and deal with his abuse. I always had it at the back of my mind that Eric could inflict great harm on me. He had, after all, said that if we broke up, he would have to kill me. Would he snap if we did break up? I have friends who dated powerful men and were similarly threatened. In some cases, the men tried to realize their threats, hiring private investigators to track the women's movements and talking about hitmen. My friends lived in mortal fear of these men and to this day they suffer from post-traumatic stress disorder (PTSD). I understand now what PTSD feels like. It's hard to describe, but David J. Morris, in his book *The Evil Hours*, explains it as "essentially a junk drawer of disconnected symptoms, which include a numbing of the emotions, hypervigilance (always being 'amped up'), social isolation, and a variety of intrusive manifestations, such as nightmares and hallucinations."

I wanted Eric to get help and for us to work things out. I thought the abuse could end. I thought, as do so many women of all types who are in these situations, that he could and would change. Yet, unless an abuser is willing to acknowledge the abuse and dig deep and do the work, he won't change.

It's not as if he didn't know he had a problem. In the spring of 2017, as things got worse, Eric told me one night that he had heard from a female friend that he had a reputation for being rough with women. I kept silent. I didn't respond. I filed the remark away in my mind.

Later, through Jane Mayer and Ronan Farrow's investigation, I would discover that in fact I was one in a long line of women who had experienced abuse by Eric Schneiderman, and that he seemed to customize the abuse, in a perhaps intuitive or feral way, with each woman. He and I didn't have a volatile relationship; we didn't have arguments. With other women, apparently, he did. He fought with them and hit them outside the bedroom. But the constant in each of his relationships was the need to hit women and dehumanize them.

Eric engaged in a pattern of abuse, and there was nothing ambiguous about it. I know I didn't trigger his sexual sadism; he was like that before I walked through the door. But he conditioned me to accept his treatment.

Eric's violent behavior in the bedroom continued to be reinforced by his frequent criticism of me, of the way I looked, my weight, what I wore, my hair. I couldn't even sit at a table and work without hearing about it. I kept trying to modulate, to be more conscientious in my appearance and my habits. But as Patricia Evans has explained, the partner of an abuser must realize "that there is no 'way she can be' to prevent the abuser from venting his anger on her. Speaking more gently, listening more attentively, being more supportive, more interesting, more learned, more fun, thinner, cuter, or classier—being more anything will not work."

In my situation, the abuse was compounded by Eric's addiction to alcohol and prescription drugs. These substances impaired his ability to function coherently and fueled his monsters. And I was the person closest to him, standing by to witness the bifurcation.

A man can't profess to be a champion of women politically and crush them privately. Eric was creating his own undoing. It was as if he were saying, "Catch me! Here I am." It was almost as if he couldn't believe his own behavior, so he had to exaggerate his position. He was laying the groundwork for the unearthing of his abuse by being so visible as an advocate for women; he was provoking the narratives of the women he had abused.

It's mind-boggling that Eric could pass laws to help women in the abstract while harming real women in his own life. His advocacy was a form of atonement but also of deflection. It was as if he were declaring, "I can't be guilty of these private crimes, because of what I do publicly."

Of course, this affliction in many men, the instinct to inflict harm on women, transcends political lines. When people have money or power or both, they can have impunity. They can be entitled. They don't have to do the right thing.

Where did this behavior come from? What was it in Eric's upbringing and experience that made him do this? I believe it came partially from his deep animus toward his mother. Eric often talked about his mother having been crazy and controlling, and he took out his pent-up hatred for her on me and other girlfriends. It is a sad, sad tale from start to finish. But being victimized as a child doesn't give anyone the right to abuse women. Eric knew he was bad, but he didn't actually want to or have the courage to deal with it.

I thought I could understand Eric: the external control versus the internal torment, the tension between how one seems and how one feels. I know what it's like to want to disappear but be unable to, to want to destroy yourself as much as you can so long as you can still stand and work and speak. You barely engage; you are constantly thinking about whether you can keep going. Eric tried to counter his addictions with meditation. But he was turning to the spiritual world with the hope that it would take away his pain without actually dealing with the pain itself.

While I was deciding whether to come forward, I watched the documentary *One of Us*, by Heidi Ewing and Rachel Grady, about the pain inflicted on people in the Hasidic community who choose to leave it. One subject, Etty, describes how her husband physically and verbally abused her, yet the local courts took their kids away from her when she divorced him. Her husband was shielded by their religious community. Her story highlighted how when women in custody battles make allegations of abuse, the judges may then punish them for making the allegations. It's almost as if the women are being told, "How dare you?" This movie had a profound impact on me. It helped me decide to speak out.

The day after my story became public, Megan McArdle, a columnist for the *Washington Post*, wrote an op-ed in response. My story had triggered her to recall being hit by a boyfriend twenty-five years before whom she stayed with for a time. She wrote about how hard it was to come forward, and how hard it was to reconcile the person who hit her with the man she loved: "You're picturing a rage-filled monster, an archetype: 'the abuser.' I'm remembering the man, who was funny and brilliant. And who was, like Schneiderman, a staunch public feminist. There were many reasons I wanted to be with him, and none of them were simple, because neither was he." Her op-ed was titled "I Went Back to a Man Who Hit Me. I'm Still Thinking About Why."

Hearing from so many people about their own experiences with abuse is what compelled me to write this book. I hope that it inspires other people to speak out, to support their friends who speak out, to be more attentive to clues. If you suspect a friend is in an abusive relationship, ask her with compassion and kindness and openness if she needs to talk. It turned out that a number of my friends thought something was wrong in my relationship but refrained from asking. If they had asked, I might have come around to telling them it was a fairy tale that had become a nightmare.

CHAPTER 7

THE NIGHTMARE

When I was a child, I often remembered and recorded my dreams. They typically were (and continue to be) coherent narratives. Sometimes I would tell my mother about a dream, and she would shush me, saying, "What nonsense." But I have always believed that dreams will tell me things if I let them. I had a dream a few months before my father died of lung cancer that my mother and I were on vacation while he lay curled up on the floor back at home. In the dream, my mother got a call from someone saying, "Dead." And my mother cried, "Daddy has died. Daddy's died. And we're not there."

Soon after having the dream, I booked a ticket to visit my family in Los Angeles and spend more time with my father. I was with him in the hospital when he died. One of the most striking memories I carry to this day is of looking into his eyes as he took his last breath. I can see his expression now in my mind. He seemed so far away.

When I was a child, I loved going to horror movies. My father took me to basically anything I wanted to see: *The Amityville Horror, Friday the 13th*. He was intrigued by my fascination with these kinds of films. He'd say, "Tanya, you're so macabre."

I enjoyed putting my hands over my eyes when the scenes got especially scary. I enjoyed jumping in my seat, the adrenaline rush. But then, afterward, at home, I would have to sleep with a light on, scared of the monsters I imagined were hiding under my bed. The nightmares felt very real.

In *The Gift of Fear*, Gavin de Becker writes about the difference between good fear and bad fear. The latter prevents us from living our best life. The former heightens our sensitivity to people, places, and things we should avoid; one might call it intuition. De Becker explains that "when it comes to danger, intuition is always right in at least two important ways: (1) It is always in response to something. (2) It always has your best interest at heart."

By the spring of 2017, I was making more and more plans to go away. When I wasn't around Eric and in his environment, there was more mental space for my intuition about him to kick in, and it was supported by my dreams.

In one of them, I was in an office with my literary agent. A woman in a suit stopped at the door and said she had heard we were speaking with a reporter about the attorney general. What could we tell her about that? We played dumb. After she left, I realized I was in danger. I told my agent to be very careful about whom she told anything to. I decided I had to pack up everything in the office, including all my clothes, and leave no trace. But I struggled to figure out where I should take everything. Where would everything be safe? I knew that I couldn't take it back to my apartment in Manhattan. There was too much risk of someone breaking in. I was especially concerned about my hard drive and computer. The dream continued with my preparing to leave the office and realizing that I was at One World Trade Center, where I was working at *Glamour*. Then the moment I was dreading arrived. Eric himself approached and asked what was going on. I pretended that nothing was happening. I tried to deflect attention from how much I had told the reporter.

I woke up. The nightmares I had started having were fatiguing.

When I went to my twenty-five-year college reunion, I felt freer and happier than I had in months. I stayed in a freshman dorm and, with my classmates, hosted all-night parties there. Many people had come with their partners and families, but I was there alone. However, word had spread about who my boyfriend was.

One friend said, "I hear you're dating a very important person."

I smiled. Inside, I thought, "Yes, I am dating an important person, but if only you knew how miserable I am."

When I returned from the reunion, Eric continued to complain about how I took up too much space. I told him I could stay at my place. Those nights I spent downtown made me realize how sleep-deprived I was, how cut off from my friends and support network I had been.

For the month of July, I went to a family wedding in Sri Lanka and then to Portland to work on a show. While I was away, when I spoke with Eric on the phone, he was always kind and calm. He said he was working on himself. He was planning to go to a meditation retreat upstate. I was hopeful that when I returned, things would be different.

The morning I arrived back in New York City, I had a shoot with Samantha Bee for *Glamour*. I mentioned Eric to her, that he was my boyfriend, and she talked about wanting to have him on her show. That night, I met Eric for dinner. He said that he was still working on himself and that he wanted space. I was actually hurt—I really did have hope that after a month apart, the peace he was feeling and the self-analysis he had engaged in while I was in Portland would have made a difference. A few weeks later, he went to another meditation retreat, and we had dinner after he returned. Again, he said he was working on himself and wanted space. At the end of the meal, I said I was going to stay at my place. He was angry that I didn't want to come home with him. Even though he had said he wanted space, he became visibly upset. He seemed like a little boy who wasn't getting his way. I felt he was treating me like a yo-yo, pushing me away and then pulling me back.

I wasn't ready to break up, but I could sense myself beginning to detach. I was focusing more on what was best for me. Still, I kept hoping that the man Eric claimed to be—a champion of women, a protector of our rights—was the person he actually was. But that wasn't the case. Eric had me in a committed relationship for almost a year. All the while, I was trying to find sense where there was none. And as we know now in painful detail, he was one of legions of powerful predatory men.

The singer R. Kelly entrapped and abused women and girls in intimate relationships for years. Michael Jackson molested children for years. Bill Cosby and Harvey Weinstein sat atop entertainment empires that gave them access to dozens of women whose lives they ruined. Judge Roy Moore preyed on girls. Donald Trump groped, grabbed, forcibly kissed, and raped women. Fox News CEO Roger Ailes, NBC host Matt Lauer, and CBS chairman and CEO Les Moonves terrorized women in their offices. Comedian Louis C.K. exposed himself to his female colleagues. Talk show host Tavis Smiley and music mogul Russell Simmons are accused of sexual misconduct by multiple women. The list is endless. These men are of different ages, colors, professions, and political leanings. What unites most of them is the impunity, denial, anger, and entitlement that characterized their reactions after being exposed. Their memories of the events are different from the victims', but their saying it wasn't true doesn't mean we can give them the benefit of the doubt.

Some of these men I had met—Weinstein on multiple occasions. During the 2017 Tribeca Film Festival, I went with Eric to a twenty-fifth-anniversary screening party for *Reservoir Dogs*. Weinstein was thrilled that such a big-shot New York state politician had taken the time to come to a party in Brooklyn. Much of the original cast was there. Ron Burkle, Weinstein's close pal and an investor in the Weinstein Company, was also there. While Eric said hi to him, I slipped away. I had heard that Burkle was an intimate terrorist whose victims were too mortally scared for their own safety to come forward.

Another time I met Weinstein was at Planned Parenthood's hundredth-anniversary gala. Eric and I were whisked to an elevated green-room area. Hillary Clinton was there, and I remember cringing as I watched her and Weinstein greet each other. She referred to him as her "old friend." Weinstein took Eric aside. He was sweating profusely and started rambling about amfAR, the AIDS charity.

"They're going to skewer me," he said to Eric. I inferred that he was referring to the press, though I didn't know what he was afraid of being skewered for.

Eric tried to calm him down and said his office would follow up with Weinstein's office to see how they could help. I think Eric enjoyed being the guy that people in power had to deal with because he had authority over their businesses and charities.

Months later, on September 23, 2017, Megan Twohey wrote in the *New York Times* about how Weinstein was being investigated for pretending to raise millions for the charity while scheming to have the money returned to a theater project of his own. Within two weeks of this article appearing, she and Jodi Kantor would break the story of Weinstein's abuse of women. *Vanity Fair's* subsequent piece about the amfAR scandal was titled "Inside Harvey Weinstein's Other Nightmare."

Another perpetrator I met—at a benefit, through a mutual friend—was Louis C.K. I remember he complimented my dress, a black-and-gold caftan, and he was perfectly nice and warm. But he and other perpetrators are bifurcated individuals. They are also narcissists with money who get off on sexually intimidating and overpowering women. And they usually have a fleet of enablers: executives, producers, agents, a whole system designed to conceal their crimes. The enablers usually wait until the perpetrators they supported go all the way down before jumping ship.

When Ivanka Trump was asked on *CBS This Morning* whether she was complicit in her father's misdeeds, she deflected. She seemed not to understand the meaning of the word. Soon thereafter, internet searches for "complicit" spiked by 11,000 percent. Women who support perpetrators are both complicit and psychologically warped. Those who stay in relationships with abusive men often do so because they are financially dependent, because they have kids and don't want to break up the family, because they don't think they will have an identity on their own, or because they enjoy the status of being the partner of a powerful man. Before I dated Eric, I had been someone who would ask, even about my own mother, "Why isn't she standing up? Why isn't she speaking out? Why isn't she running away?" And then it happened to me, and I got it.

Fairly soon after I realized that I was caught in a vicious cycle of abuse, I started telling people, out of self-preservation, about my experiences with Eric. But I was scared what he might do if I left him. When I opened up, I finally had people responding that it was not okay, that I needed to run. One friend connected me with a domestic violence expert and lawyer, Jennifer Friedman. She and I spoke on the phone, and I described my experience. It took my confiding in her for me to see that Eric was never going to change and that he had probably done this to other women.

I finally told my therapist, Dr. Mark Epstein, about the abuse. I had been telling him all along the way about Eric's drinking and his controlling behavior, about how I was feeling sleep-deprived. He had encouraged me to spend more time away from Eric. Then, as soon as I told him about the physical abuse (around the time I had spoken with Friedman), he said I had to get out.

During that session with Mark, I asked him, "What do you really think about all this?"

He said, "He's a pig." He also said that he was sad for me because he had been excited about the relationship. He felt bad that he hadn't been able to help me earlier.

I said, "Well, I told you about the drinking, controlling, criticism, and sleep deprivation, but I didn't tell you for almost a year about everything else that was happening."

He said, "And that's an important part of the story. I have patients who wait seven years to tell me about their sexual abuse as a child."

Until then, I had been scared to tell anyone because I knew the situation was wrong and because I thought Eric would get better. As for my psychology, I would liken it to having Stockholm syndrome. The term was first used in 1973, after a bank robbery in Sweden, when the hostages developed a bizarre empathy with their captors and wouldn't testify against them during the trial. Today, Stockholm syndrome is used to describe a range of scenarios in which people identify with someone who has committed an act of wrongdoing against them. Actress Salma Hayek wrote an op-ed for the *New York Times* titled "Harvey Weinstein Is My Monster Too" in which she used the term:

> He told me that the only thing I had going for me was my sex appeal and that there was none of that in [*Frida*]. So he told me he was going to shut down the film because no one would want to see me in that role. It was soul crushing because, I confess, lost in the fog of a sort of Stockholm syndrome, I wanted him to see me as an artist.

In my case, I also felt that if I talked about the physical abuse, it would become real. In *No Visible Bruises: What We Don't Know About Domestic Violence Can Kill Us*, Rachel Louise

Snyder writes, "[Physical abuse] is most often hidden from even one's closest confidantes, and on many occasions the physical violence is far less damaging than the emotional and verbal violence."

I had tried to deal with Eric directly to turn things around. When I talked with him about the physical and sexual violence, he made it seem like a game, even though I told him it didn't feel good and I didn't like it. When I talked with him about the verbal and psychological abuse, he was aware of it but had excuses: he was depressed; times were turbulent; he was going to get help; he was going to work on himself. I would cling to the hope that he was telling the truth, but as Patricia Evans explains, "the first stage of recognition is the beginning of the partner's change from doubting herself to doubting her mate."

I've lived through nightmares before. When my former husband left me, I felt abandoned. I didn't know which way was up. The intensity of his cruelty, especially so soon after my surgeries, hurt me severely. He agreed to go to a couples counselor. After the first session, the counselor asked me, cautiously, "Tanya, do you think there's someone else?" At the time, I didn't know for sure, though I suspected. And of course, it was later confirmed that he was indeed already with someone else, the woman whom so many friends had warned me about.

The situation with my ex-husband felt like boilerplate romantic troubles compared to the nightmare I was engulfed in with Eric. The panic attacks, the heart palpitations, the spontaneous shaking—they are all terrifying. And his position of legal and political power only heightened my fear. He was a New York state politician with a big national profile who was increasingly seen as a savior of democracy. Moreover, if the president of the United States was not being held accountable as a perpetrator of sexual violence, how could I expect Eric to be?

In 2018, the W. M. Keck Center for Collaborative Neuroscience at Rutgers University released a study about stressful life memories related to ruminative thoughts in women with histories of sexual violence. In the piece, published in *Frontiers in Psychiatry*, coauthors Emma Millon, Han Yan Chang, and Tracy Shors write, "More than one in every four women in the world experience sexual violence (SV) in their lifetime, most often as teenagers and young adults. These traumatic experiences leave memories in the brain, which are difficult if not impossible to forget."

Subsequently, Jessica Ravitz and Arman Azad explained in an article for CNN, "Memories That Last: What Sexual Assault Survivors Remember and Why," "Victims of sexual violence reported 44% more depressive symptoms and twice as many symptoms of anxiety than those who had no history with sexual violence." As the Keck Center study showed, women who've experienced a sexual assault are more likely to remember their assault than other sorts of trauma, such as car accidents. When Bill Cosby was sent to prison, one of his accusers, Andrea Constand, wrote in a victim impact statement, "Bill Cosby took my beautiful, healthy young spirit and crushed it. He robbed me of my health and vitality, my open nature, and my trust in myself and others."

It took me a while to open up to friends and experts and to realize that I needed to figure out how to get out. I worried that those around Eric would have his back if I made accusations against him. I needed to protect myself.

I thought, "I'm brave, but I'm also fragile."

After I connected with Jennifer Friedman, I had more of the tools I needed to extricate myself from my relationship with Eric as gently as possible without setting him off. With her help, I began to make a plan.

CHAPTER 8

WHAT IS INTIMATE VIOLENCE?

Until I experienced intimate partner violence, I didn't understand it. Even after I started experiencing it, it took me a while to name it. I had a hard time opening up to friends, but when I did—and especially after my story became public—I witnessed an outpouring from friends and even strangers. Nobody talks about it until somebody else talks about it.

When I asked Rachna Khare of Daya Houston (an organization for South Asian victims of abuse) for her definition of the issue, she responded, "Intimate partner violence is a pattern of abusive behavior used to maintain power and control over a partner. The abuse can be physical, emotional, verbal, sexual, or financial—to name a few. Intimate partner violence can occur in any kind of intimate relationship."

"Intimate violence" is a subset of domestic and intimate partner violence. It happens during sex and is entwined with other patterns of abuse. According to the World Health Organization, "Research suggests that physical violence in intimate relationships is often accompanied by psychological abuse, and in one-third to over one-half of cases by sexual abuse."

Intimate violence is very much part of the patriarchy. Brittney Cooper has written that "patriarchy is nothing if not the structurally induced hatred of women." What makes this violence so insidious is that the victim might not immediately realize it's wrong. The abuser can manipulate the victim into thinking their behavior in the bedroom is acceptable. But even in consensual sexual relationships, lines can be crossed. The entire construct of consent is at risk of becoming warped in domestic situations. What is the difference between consenting and withstanding?

Although intimate violence affects both women and men, in both opposite-sex and same-sex relationships—and I touch upon various configurations—I focus here mostly on women in relationship to men. But the takeaways from this book can be universally applied.

The vast majority of violence is committed by men. According to FBI records of ten-year arrest trends between 2008 and 2017, 87 percent of murders and nonnegligent manslaughters, 97 percent of rapes, and 76.8 percent of aggravated assaults were committed by men. Globally, almost 30 percent of women have experienced intimate partner violence, and as much as 38 percent of murders of women are committed by a male intimate partner.

Before I met Eric, I had often considered what I would do if I were attacked by a man. I had envisioned situations in which I might be ambushed, either in the woods near my place in Portland, Oregon, or walking down a dark street to my apartment in New York City. I imagined that I would start screaming like a banshee, kick the guy in the balls, yell at the top of my lungs, and flail my arms around as if I were possessed.

But here I was acquiescing to abuse in the home, at the hands of someone I knew.

A World Health Organization report on intimate partner violence outlined some of the reasons why women don't leave violent relationships: fear of retaliation, lack of alternative means of economic support, and concern for their children. Community and societal factors, such as gender-inequitable social norms that link manhood with dominance and aggression, also play a part.

Women are blamed for staying and blamed for fighting back. They're blamed for getting into the relationship in the first place. That happened to me—a friend said I should really think about what it was about me that had allowed me to get involved with Eric. It wasn't helpful for her to say that, but I forgave her for it. I also thought, "His behavior had been going on for a very long time. I stopped it."

Rachna Khare asked me, "Why do we question victims of intimate partner violence in a way we do not with victims of other crimes?" She also said, "Society continues to blame the victim in a way we would never dream of doing for other violent crimes. My personal opinion is that society is afraid to admit that intimate partner violence can happen to any of us. Instead, we try to find ways to placate ourselves. We find false causes to explain violence so that we can put our heads in the sand and say, 'I would never be in that situation.'"

On May 7, 2018, my story of intimate violence became public in an exposé by Jane Mayer and Ronan Farrow in the *New Yorker*. Before then, I had been known for my work, my advocacy for the rights and safety of women and children, my art. When I wrote *The Big Lie*, about my fertility struggles, I was largely in control of the narrative. But here, the story and my character were being spun by outlet after outlet in a way over which I had no control.

Something else happened as well. As I opened up to friends, ones I'd known for years, they told me for the first time details about their own experiences of being abused: one whose boyfriend broke her rib, another whose ex-husband would push her hard against a wall in front of their children. A young director in her twenties whom I was mentoring told me about a housemate who got drunk and assaulted her. One friend was dependent on her husband to drive her. She knew how to drive, but he made sure that she didn't get a chance to do it. They had only one car and lived in a town where there was no other way to get around. She said the physical abuse usually happened in the car, when he literally had control of the keys. After she got him arrested during an especially violent fight, he told her from jail that he'd given her address and phone number to fellow inmates who were murderers and soon to be released. She slept with a butcher knife under her bed.

The stories involved varying degrees of violence, but what united them was the trauma inflicted, the violence not recipro-cated, the fear, the self-blame. The Me Too movement inherits thousands of years of women and their bodies being consid-ered dispensable. Many people would rather that women suffer than speak their truths. But we need to talk about these things because as long as we don't, the perpetrators can and will get away with them. Just because they're not doing these things the majority of the time doesn't mean we have to tolerate their actions. Just because they may have performed some good deeds doesn't mean they get a pass. They have to be called out.

I remember numerous times I avoided or got out of threatening sexual situations with a man. When I was walking near my high school, a man in a light-blue suit standing in the bushes pulled down his pants and exposed himself to me. When I was in my twenties, a director insisted on seeing me naked before casting me. When I was in my thirties, at a bar, a married actor said nonchalantly that he wanted me to come to his hotel and sit on his face. After I didn't, I heard he got into a fight with a hotel concierge.

One thing is very clear: As with so many issues we keep hidden away, women have to talk to one another about the horrible ways in which we are treated. We are taught to be scared. We are conditioned to shut up. But we have to share our stories with one another and the world so we can shape the public discourse. And women need to take over not just the discourse but the world.

Every day, there seems to be a new story about a predator or a predatory system that preys on women, about perpetrators committing intimate terrorism. It's easy to get caught up in the noise and horror of each revelation. We might think it doesn't bother us until we hear another person's story, and then we are triggered. It is important to identify what we can do to change the future.

In February 2018, I attended a conversation hosted by PEN America about the Me Too movement. The panelists talked about how some of those denounced in the current climate were their friends and colleagues. However, taking a utilitarian approach, some suggested that if thousands of women were saved by the outing of serious perpetrators, it might not matter if a few innocent men were unfairly taken down.

This struck me as dangerous thinking. Accusations can happen fast and in a sweeping way, and we should avoid witch hunts. Due process is vital to fairness. I believe in investigating allegations. Jane Mayer has written about how the failure to look thoroughly into the allegations against Al Franken resulted in his resignation as a US senator before it was discovered that the story told by his accuser, Leeann Tweeden, was full of holes. Mayer's article about Franken in the *New Yorker* caused great controversy, but if we don't establish the veracity of the allegations and the credibility of the accuser, if we don't distinguish between men behaving badly and men committing horrific acts against women that cause lifelong trauma, we do the Me Too movement a great disservice.

Abusers such as PBS talk show host Charlie Rose thrived for decades despite many people knowing about their depravity. How do we make victims feel that they will be protected and it is safe to come forward? We have to dismantle thousands of years of patriarchy. That might take thousands more years to achieve, but we can take measures now through education, legislation, and representation.

At the PEN panel, the writer Masha Gessen suggested that it might be better to have less sex than one bad sexual encounter. But, she asserted, we should end this conversation with the feeling that we should have more, not less, sex. I myself am not advocating for sexual puritanism. The spectrum of desire is broad and should allow for a variety of experiences. This book is about prioritizing the needs and safety of the woman in a sexual relationship as much as the man. It's about taking misogyny out of the bedroom. My intent is not to stifle experimentation; it is to prevent harm and trauma. That involves communication. It involves questions and cues. It involves mutual respect.

Eric was so effective at tailoring his abuse of me that I thought I was responsible for it, that something about me had encouraged it. Ultimately, I discovered not only that his abuse was *not* specific to me but also that I was part of a pattern that had gone on for years and years. In addition to the women whose accounts were depicted in the *New Yorker*, there were multiple women who reached out to the publication after the story came out. They wanted to talk about their own horrible experiences with him.

Jess McIntosh, a Democratic strategist, published her own account about Eric. I knew McIntosh but became aware of her experience with him only when I read about it on Elle.com. While she was a researcher on his state senator campaign, thirteen years before, he turned a meeting into a date. Even though she kept saying she had a boyfriend, he kept making moves on her. She was twenty-three; he was fifty. After some making out, she abruptly got out of the car, breaking a string of her grandmother's pearls. In the piece, she writes, "The truth is that story doesn't have a damn thing to do with me, and maybe that's the worst part. Sometimes we're just at the mercy of the men who decide what's next for us: whether we get hit that night, whether we get home."

Shortly before my story came out, I was with a group of friends who were helping me prepare for tough questions that might come my way from reporters. They asked me to describe explicitly the violence in the bedroom. One friend there had recently broken up with her boyfriend, partially because he was an addict. Later that day, she called and said, "You could have been describing what happened to me."

A male friend told me his story of witnessing domestic violence as a child, when he would watch his father beat his mother mercilessly. That friend's partner told me, "His mother could have been dead given what his dad did to her." Of the one in fifteen children exposed to intimate partner violence each year, 90 percent are eyewitnesses to it. I am among that 90 percent. Meanwhile, numerous friends have told me about grandfathers, uncles, other relatives, and family friends who molested or raped them when they were children. This sexually abusive behavior is passed down from generation to generation. These cycles are perpetuated without repercussion except for the trauma that victims carry within themselves for the rest of their lives, and some victims go on to become the next generation of abusers.

But there are stories that end with redemption. My cousin told me about a lawyer friend who was harassed by a partner at her firm. When she complained, the firm told her that something was wrong with her and that she should go to therapy. Instead, she got a lawyer and received a five-hundred-thousand-dollar settlement. Jennifer Friedman, the domestic violence expert I spoke to, worked with a human trafficking victim who had been promised a great job but instead became a slave in a Nigerian diplomat's home in Westchester, New York. She escaped and became an advocate for human trafficking victims in her community upstate.

Sharon White-Harrigan, a prison reform activist, turned her deeply painful history into a vocation. When White-

Harrigan was sixteen, the father of her child died in a car crash three weeks before their wedding. She turned to an older male friend for support. They became lovers, and he began abusing her, giving her black eyes and bruised lips. Years after that relationship ended, another man attempted to rape her, but she was determined not to let him overpower her. She stabbed him and got away. When he died later that night, she turned herself in. She talked about how she was assigned to a racist judge who didn't see her as a victim but as another black woman he thought should be in jail. She was sent to Bedford Hills Correctional Facility, in Westchester County, New York, where she would spend the next eleven years. There, she found that most of the female inmates had experienced sexual abuse and violence. White-Harrigan studied through a Women's Prison Association educational program, and after her release, she earned a master's in clinical social work. She became an advocate for women in prison who shouldn't be there and worked to prevent them from getting caught up in the criminal justice system in the first place. In her case, redemption did not mean that she got a second chance, because she was never given a first chance. It meant that she forgave the world and contributed to making it a better place even though it had cruelly turned its back on her.

Gavin de Becker has written about how he grew up watching his father beat his mother, and how his mother was a heroin addict who eventually shot his father. Dealing with the violence and fear in his childhood inspired de Becker to devote his career to ensuring the safety of others. He has worked as a private security expert for royalty, celebrities, politicians, and billionaires. For the general public, de Becker has provided resources and has written books such as *The Gift of Fear*, which should be required reading for everyone. When I myself read his book, I was especially affected by the chapter on "intimate enemies"—it could have been written about my relationship with Eric in its depiction of the intimidation, verbal abuse, controlling behavior, and alcohol-fueled violence that can occur between intimate partners.

Abuse permeates all aspects of society: farms and factories; schools, prisons, and restaurants; the judiciary and government. Abuse that happens in the outside world often begins at home. With the Me Too and TIME'S UP movements, the focus has been more on the workplace and one-off experiences, and less on the home and serial domestic violence. But home is where these behaviors become conditioned, and until we address that root cause, we will never do away with violence in the workplace, violence in public; we will never do away with war.

David Remnick, in a *New Yorker* article, examined the implications post-Weinstein for powerful men, including the president, when it comes to their history of abuse. He cited Susan Brownmiller's 1975 book, *Against Our Will: Men, Women, and Rape*: "Man's discovery that his genitalia could serve as a weapon to generate fear must rank as one of the most important discoveries of prehistoric times, along with the use of fire and the first crude stone axe." He continued: "Sexual coercion, and the threat of its possibility, in the street, in the workplace, and in the home, she found, is less a matter of frenzied lust than a deliberate exercise of physical power, a declaration of superiority 'designed to intimidate and inspire fear.'"

I have often wondered about how terrifying it would be

for men if women could fight back, if they could protect themselves and one another with their bodies alone. Naomi Alderman imagined such a world in her 2016 novel *The Power*. After discovering their hidden physical abilities, women take over in various countries around the world where they had been previously enslaved and oppressed, from Saudi Arabia to India to, yes, the United States.

In 2018, a Thomson Reuters survey placed the United States as the tenth most dangerous place in the world for women, the only Western country on that list. (India was number one.) This ranking of the United States stretches across all aspects of the American canvas. The equality and safety of all American women cannot be achieved while that fact holds. But how do we counter it when we have a predator in the highest office in the land and multiple predators on the Supreme Court?

In a February 2018 article for the *Guardian*, Jessica Valenti pointed out that the White House at the time was stacked with domestic abusers: former chief strategist Steve Bannon, former staff secretary Rob Porter, the president himself. Bannon had been charged with domestic violence and battery in 1996, after his then wife called 911. Porter had been accused of assaulting both his ex-wives and a former girlfriend. The president had been credibly accused by more than a dozen women of sexual assault, groping, or harassment, as well as of a horrific rape by his ex-wife (although Ivana Trump later backtracked on this accusation). (In 2019, E. Jean Carroll added her name to the list of those accusing Trump of rape.) And let us not forget the 2017 sexual assault accusation against former campaign manager Corey Lewandowski, domestic violence accusations against labor secretary nominee Andrew Puzder, and the president's endorsement of Roy Moore, an accused pedophile, for senator of Alabama. These facts don't send a message to women that they are protected by those at the top.

Where do we go from here? We have to chip away at the power that keeps these men in place. We have to chip away at the conditioning and behavior that gives rise to the devastating statistics. Although the overall number of Americans sexually assaulted fell by more than half from 1993 to 2016, the Department of Justice's 2013–2017 National Crime Victimization Survey stated that according to 2017 data, an American was sexually assaulted every ninety-two seconds. RAINN (Rape, Abuse, Incest National Network), the largest anti-sexual violence organization in the country, has shown how different populations have been affected by these assaults. As of 2019, 60,000 children each year are victims of "substantiated or indicated" sexual abuse; among the general public, each year 321,500 Americans twelve and older are sexually assaulted or raped. Moreover, sexual violence affects mostly women (nine out of ten rape victims), with most assaults occurring in or near their homes.

RAINN also cites that 80,600 prison inmates are sexually assaulted or raped each year. On top of this statistic was the epidemic of "Hazing, Humiliation, Terror" for female workers in prisons that Caitlin Dickerson wrote about for the *New York Times*. "Some inmates do not stop at stares. They also grope, threaten and expose themselves. But what is worse . . . male colleagues can and do encourage such behavior, undermining the authority of female officers and jeopardizing their safety. Other male employees join in the harassment themselves."

Another statistic provided by RAINN is that 18,900 military personnel experience unwanted sexual contact each year. In "40 Stories from Women About Life in the Military," an article by Lauren Katzenberg for the *New York Times*, naval Petty Officer First Class Liberty Law said:

> In 2006, a male shipmate got into my barracks room and placed a camera in my bathroom and set it to record. I found it only after getting out of the shower. I took the camera to my male chief, whom I had known for only about a month. He assured me that he would get to the bottom of it. By lunchtime, the strange looks from everyone became obvious. Another shipmate told me that everyone in the company office had passed the camera around and saw the video of me naked, getting into and out of the shower.

In March 2019, Senator Martha McSally, an Arizona Republican who was the first female fighter pilot to fly in combat, spoke publicly about being raped by a superior officer and sexually assaulted multiple times while she was serving her country. In testimony to the Senate Armed Services Subcommittee, she said, "I thought I was strong, but felt powerless. The perpetrators abused their position of power in profound ways." At first, she kept quiet because she "didn't trust the system at the time." And when she started talking about her experiences, she "felt like the system was raping [her] all over again."

Migrants and immigrants face particularly dangerous situations. In a story subtitled "The Hidden Nightmare of Sexual Violence at the Border," for the *New York Times*,

Manny Fernandez wrote that a review of police reports and court records in Arizona, California, New Mexico, and Texas showed "more than 100 documented reports of sexual assault of undocumented women along the border in the past two decades, a number that most likely only skims the surface." In addition, "the federal government over a recent four-year period has received more than 4,500 complaints about the sexual abuse of immigrant children at government-funded detention facilities." Two teenage girls were sexually assaulted by a Customs and Border Protection officer, "who they said forced them to strip, fondled them, then tried to get them to stop crying by offering chocolates, potato chips and a blanket."

For transgender people, the statistics are also disturbing. "Forty-seven percent of transgender people report being sexually assaulted at some point in their lives, both in and out of the workplace." In addition, the CDC has declared same-sex domestic violence an epidemic. Its report "found that bisexual women had an overwhelming prevalence of violent partners in their lives: seventy-five percent had been with a violent partner, as opposed to forty-six percent of lesbian women and forty-three percent of straight women. For bisexual men, that number was forty-seven percent. For gay men, it was forty percent, and twenty-one percent for straight men."

Intimate partner violence has been linked to a wide range of negative health outcomes, including depression, post-traumatic stress and other anxiety disorders, sleep difficulties, eating disorders, and suicide attempts. Rachel Louise Snyder highlights the obstacles to dealing with this epidemic in *No Visible Bruises*:

The United States spends as much as twenty-five times more on researching cancer or heart disease than it does on violence prevention despite the enormous costs of violence to our communities. A 2018 study published in the *American Journal of Preventive Medicine* put the cost of intimate partner violence at nearly $3.6 trillion ... [T]his equates to $2 trillion in medical costs and $73 billion in criminal justice expenses, among other costs like lost productivity or property damage. Intimate partner violence costs women $103K and men $23K over the course of a single lifetime.

Discussing "An Indigenous Response to #MeToo," a film made for *Rematriation* magazine, Dr. Hayley Marama Cavino, a Māori tribeswoman (of the tribes Ngāti Pūkenga/Ngāti Whitikaupeka) and professor at Syracuse University, explains, "One of our elders at home—Mereana Pitman—says that when you violate women and children you violate everyone, including yourself, because of the ways we are interconnected through genealogy. Sexual violence is never—for us—only about what happens to the individual, but rather is an assault against the blood—against our ancestors, our children to come, and all with whom we are connected in present time and place."

Like Mereana Pitman, many people simply want justice, safety, and bodily autonomy—all of which include an end to intimate violence. But others won't give up the status quo. We are in a war that will lead us to one of two possible outcomes: a world that is less safe for women or a world that is safer for women. I am fighting for the latter.

CHAPTER 9

EXTRACTION

In September 2017, a friend gifted me with a visit to a medium, a person who communicates with the dead. I had never been to one before. As a child in Sri Lanka, I became accustomed to astrologers and psychics; that form of spirituality was normal, but I always took it with a grain of salt. When I was young, my mother had my horoscope read. I wish I still had that booklet with predictions about my life. I remember it said I would become a doctor and have two children.

Going to this medium, as an adult, I was intrigued but skeptical. My friend sent me because she wanted to do something nice for me and thought I would enjoy it. I had read Laura Lynne Jackson's *The Light Between Us*, about her experience as a medium. Jackson had worked with parents grieving the loss of a child and with law enforcement agents seeking clues to the location of the body of a murder victim. I kind of knew what to expect, but I wasn't prepared for the specificity of the reading.

Before I left to meet the medium, on a whim, I took three small photos I kept near my bed and put them in my backpack. They were of important people in my life who had died: my grandfather, my father, and a friend who had been killed by a hit-and-run driver when I was in high school. I believe that people who leave this earth still walk with us. I was curious how the presence of these three photos might impact what the medium saw.

Soon after she began, she asked, "Are you heartbroken?"

I responded, "I think so."

She talked about how I had been knocked off my center. She felt a tensing in her chest. She told me to be really careful, to tiptoe through this time.

She said, "If it hasn't already, it's gonna get a little messy." About the man in my life, she said, "I don't like him for you. There's a bigger situation here that's going to lead you out of this. I keep hearing the word *deafening*."

I had been experiencing a ringing in my ears. I didn't know where it had come from. I wondered if this was what she meant.

"There's a very slight man who walks with you"—a man with the same physicality as me. She said that he's guiding me through this time. "It's your father."

Suddenly, she said, "There's somebody showing me a necklace with a gold elephant on it. That's just a confirmation."

A few days before I had this reading, I had opened my jewelry drawer to find a gold chain to replace one that had broken. The necklace I found was one I hadn't looked at in years, and it had a gold elephant on it. The drawer was just to the right of where the photos I put in my backpack had been.

After she mentioned this necklace, I settled in to receive everything she wanted to tell me.

"You're going to experience a detachment from things, to push them away, without the guilt, without the weight."

I told her, "I could potentially be in danger."

She said, "I don't like him. He's not well. He's not well, mentally." She talked about how he was a man of ego, charisma, and addiction. She said that any contact with him would rattle me right now, and that I needed to be protected. She said to ghost him, but to make it seem like I was focusing on myself and my work.

I said, "As I piece together events in the last year, I see a lot of moments of abuse."

"This isn't going to get better. He does not have a turn-around in his future. You need to get help from people who know what you're going through." She said to make sure they were people who had no connection to him, that it couldn't get back to him what I was thinking.

I told the medium, "But I've also seen the softer side of him."

"Fuck it. Don't worry about the soft side. You have the power; you have the information. The more people in your pod that know, the safer you are. When you tell someone about this sort of abuse, you make it less okay. You need to tell somebody what he did, and you need to see the reaction in their eyes. You need to let the air out of the balloon."

She talked about someone showing her a big bouquet of bright flowers, a woman who left us earlier than she should have, a tall white woman with long white hair who bit her nails. That was my friend in the photo in my backpack.

"She's well. She's where she's supposed to be. She's also the one you can talk to during this time in particular. She's a totem for you. She wants you to plan a path to joy." She continued, "There's an honoring of the hurt that you're not very good at."

She told me to be careful about the stress of the road I was about to travel. Then she talked about a man surrounded by numbers who paid attention to the smallest details and used his hands a lot. That was my grandfather, a masterful accountant who folded his clothes meticulously. She said my grandfather wanted me to make the following lists:

- People I would tell
- People who would know what to do
- Things that were better before my relationship
- Things that I'd stopped myself from doing
- Things I would tell the person I loved the most if they were in my position
- Things I wanted in a partner

She also told me to put on paper every remote trace of pain that I'd been through, even if I realized later on that I saw it in the flash of an eye.

When I returned home, I sat at my desk and started the lists. For the things I would tell a person I loved the most who was in this position, I wrote:

- Stay away.
- There's nothing to be gained by confronting him.
- Surround yourself with people who have your back.
- Don't worry about those who don't have your back.
- You are more important than him.

As I completed these lists, I sobbed.

Around that time, I got together with my longtime friend Danzy Senna, an author who was in town for the Brooklyn

Book Festival. Over dinner, I told her about how things had been spiraling downward over the last many months with Eric. As I described the details of the abuse, she became disturbed. I told her Eric was at a meditation retreat. She offered to go with me right then and there to get all my belongings from his place. I had the keys; we could have done it. But I told her I wanted to wait. My things were not important.

The next day, I went to Los Angeles for a *Glamour* Women of the Year shoot with Nicole Kidman, who in *Big Little Lies* plays a woman dealing with intimate violence in the sexual context. During the interview, as she said the words "domestic violence," my phone rang, displaying "No Caller ID." I knew it was Eric. It was a sign from the universe. I hadn't spoken with him in over a week—the last time I had seen him was when I went by his place to get my Mass General ID card and he criticized my perfume. I had already begun the process of drifting. What did he want? My body tensed up. My heart started palpitating.

He called twice more in the next twenty-four hours, increasingly agitated in his messages by the fact that he couldn't reach me. He thought we were supposed to have dinner that week and wanted to confirm. By the third time he called, I thought it would make him crazy if I didn't respond, so I sent a short email to say that I was traveling and couldn't get together with him.

Meanwhile, I continued to speak with Jennifer Friedman. She kept reminding me that my safety, not his career, was paramount. She wasn't worried for my safety in public, but she recognized that I was on a slippery slope.

She said, "He's lived a double life for all these years. If

you're alone with him, we don't know what he's capable of. I don't want you to be alone with him. Don't poke the bear."

Friedman and I talked about getting an order of protection, but Eric's prominent position made it impossible to do anything outside the public spotlight. She explained that as the attorney general of New York State, he would find out in three seconds if I filed a petition. She was really worried about my being alone with him because, she said, "that was always his MO." She cited the violence that happened during sex—always behind closed doors, only in very private spaces. Friedman and I both agreed that the purpose of an order of protection, to keep him away from me, would not necessarily solve the problems in my situation. She wanted me not to ruffle his feathers, to get out smoothly, without alarming him. She encouraged me to slowly fade out of his life and treat it more like a normal breakup. Afterward, she and I would talk about next steps.

At the time, I had no desire to go public. I had my friends, my work, my family. Furthermore, I had my home, my own apartment. I thought about the devastating statistics on domestic violence victims and homelessness: the fact that 63 percent of homeless women in the United States are survivors of domestic violence. But I had a place to escape to. I could focus on recovering and getting on with my life.

Eric really wanted to talk to me. Yom Kippur was about to begin, and he wrote to me that he was going to use the period of atonement to reflect. After my conversations with Jennifer Friedman, I thought I could handle speaking with Eric and, moreover, use the opportunity to extricate myself. He and I set up a time for a call on October 1, after the end of Yom Kippur.

I consulted with Friedman about how to prepare. She told me not to say yes to anything that would involve seeing him, like having dinner. She told me to say, "I need to think about it." She warned me that he knew my strengths and weaknesses. Don't give away anything, she said. Don't be impulsive. Don't agree to go to his place by yourself. She wanted me to know that I was blameless, that his behavior was not my fault. He had made me feel responsible for his well-being. He might believe that I was responsible, but he had lived a long life before I entered the picture. Friedman said that I needed to be "unbrainwashed" of his psychological manipulation.

We came up with scripts for various scenarios. I'd been avoiding him for so many weeks that it would be odd if he hadn't picked up on where things were heading—that is, toward the end of our relationship. But she said he might initiate the breakup conversation, which would be ideal. That way, he would have agency over the situation. By giving him control, I could more easily extricate myself in such a way that he felt that he was his own boss and that he was still in charge of me. If that occurred, I could simply say, "I think that's for the best."

If he didn't initiate the breakup, I could say, "This just isn't working for me anymore," or "This isn't working for either one of us. It's not bringing out the best in either of us." If he tried to criticize me or the call took a negative turn, I should exit as quickly as possible.

"When people come at you, you get tongue-tied. It's a strategic way to manipulate and weaken you," she said.

She told me to be detached, be strong, and take control of the conversation. We decided that I could say, "I recognize how hard this is for both of us, but I need to end the conversation," or "I'm sorry, I just can't have a conversation when you're criticizing me."

She wanted me to identify a friend I could see after I spoke with him, so that I wouldn't be alone.

When the time came for him to call, I calmed my nerves. I had a plan.

He started with, "It seems like you've been avoiding me."

I responded, "I just need time."

He said that maybe we should go our separate ways.

I said the line I had practiced with Jennifer Friedman: "I think that would be for the best."

He asked, surprised, "Really?"

I said, "Yes, I'll be fine."

Without drama, we agreed by phone to break up.

Four days later, the Harvey Weinstein story broke in the *New York Times*. I felt a wave crash around me. The #MeToo reckoning had begun. On October 10, when the *New Yorker* published its Weinstein story by Ronan Farrow, Eric emailed me, "When you can, I think we should talk. I want to continue to support your good work." I didn't think the timing was a coincidence.

That week, he wrote me twice more, first telling me that he would be away for the weekend if I wanted to come by and get my things, and then asking if he should come with me to the *Glamour* awards.

I responded, "Thank you for this offer. I am not going to get to that this weekend. I don't think it would be the best idea for you to come to the gala."

My Me Too situation was happening concurrently with

developments in the national news cycle, and I felt overwhelmed by the convergence. I spoke with Jennifer Friedman,
who said she had been thinking about me as the Weinstein
news erupted. She was still concerned about my safety. She
asked about the security in my building. We talked again about
an order of protection, but I felt that it would become public
and there would be no way to protect my confidentiality. Also,
I was not interested in ruining Eric's career. Friedman said that
Eric's duplicitousness reminded her of Eliot Spitzer, the former governor of New York who had resigned in disgrace over
his solicitation of prostitutes.

We talked about how the next step would be to retrieve
my belongings from Eric's apartment. Friedman had twenty
years of experience working with survivors; she understood the
way an abuser's mind worked. I told her I still had the keys to
Eric's apartment. Could I just go get everything when I knew
he wouldn't be home? She wondered whether, if he came back
to an empty apartment, he would fly off the handle. My stuff
was not the most important thing; most important was being
safe. She advised me against going over there anytime soon, and
that when I did, I should make sure that a friend went with me.

I wrote in my journal:

> If you want to kill me, go ahead. I've already faced death.
> You want to tap my phones? Fine. I already assumed all
> my communications are being tracked.
> You want to put me in jail? Go ahead.

Soon thereafter, Jennifer Gonnerman and I met for dinner
on the Lower East Side. I hadn't seen her in a few months; she

and her husband had had dinner with me and Eric early in our relationship. At that time, things were good. Before Jennifer and I met this time, I anticipated telling her what was going on now. I wasn't sure how.

But she opened the door, asking, "So, is Eric going to send Harvey to jail?" She meant Weinstein.

I took a deep breath and said, "Jen, there's something I have to tell you that isn't easy."

After I told her what had been going on and mentioned that my next step was simply to get my things at his place, she offered to come with me.

I wrote to Eric asking if I could come by that Friday. He said I could. I asked if I should leave the key with his doorman, but he said I didn't have to, that he would get it from me another time.

Jen and another friend came with me, and we worked quickly to round up my belongings. The book *On Tyranny*, by Timothy Snyder, was on the dining table. A framed tweet by the president attacking Eric, which he had received when he was on *Late Night with Seth Meyers*, was nearby.

Jen told me to take photos of the different rooms in the apartment. She said that one day I might want to refer to them to spark details and memories of what had happened to me there. As an investigative reporter, she knew the advice to give.

After we had left the building and were waiting for a cab, with bags and bags of my things next to us on the sidewalk, she said to me, "You can't be the first person he has done this to. Someone doesn't just wake up in the morning and exhibit these behaviors."

CHAPTER 10

THE PATTERN

11:11—that was the time on the clock as I walked through my front door after bringing my things back from his place. Whenever I see 11:11, I make a wish. This particular time, I wished to be safe.

The next morning, I received a text from Jennifer Gonnerman: "I have some info. Can you talk?" I called her right away. She was with a childhood friend of her husband. He just happened to be in town that day, and he was hanging out with her family in the park. Jennifer knew the friend had worked with an ex-girlfriend of Eric's. She didn't know if he and Eric's ex had been good friends or if they were still in touch, but Jennifer casually asked him if he had ever heard the ex say anything about Eric Schneiderman.

Without skipping a beat, the man talked about his friend dating Eric and about Eric's slapping her and spitting at her in bed. It turned out that the man was still in touch with the woman and, in fact, they were quite close. He called her while Jennifer was on the phone with me. He told her what the woman was saying, and Jennifer conveyed the messages to me:

Eric would tell this woman to get Botox. He insulted her ankles; he said they were thick. If they weren't, he said, she'd be really intimidating. It was a long time before me that she had been with him. She wanted me to know that I wasn't alone and I wasn't crazy. She also said to call her if I wanted to talk.

After I hung up with Jennifer, my heart dropped, and I felt panicked. He was going to do to someone else what he had done to this woman and to me, and I felt a moral obligation to prevent that from happening. But how could I do so without putting myself in danger? Jennifer Friedman had made it clear that confronting him might set him off.

Another friend reached out to tell me that she had heard from a mutual friend about a woman who used to work for Eric. The gist of it was that the woman found him extremely creepy—always rescheduling an afternoon work meeting to an after-work drinks thing. He would be very suggestive in conversation, and she was wary of him as a result.

I spent the next twenty-four hours intensely deliberating. I was part of a pattern: I was not the first, and I wouldn't be the last. It would be easier to drift away and not say anything. But that wouldn't be me. Discovering that others could be in danger marked a turning point for me. I wondered, "Who's next?" The silence of women before me meant that I had suffered, too, and silence didn't feel like an option I could live with. I felt that I was in a lose-lose situation.

Trauma can be so deafening at times that it becomes hard to think. In my case, the decision to fade away quietly and let Eric do his work conflicted with my desire to prevent him from harming another woman. I thought the world needed him to do a few more good things, such as stop Trump's travel bans and protect transgender people in the military. What made my situation complex and different was that my abuser was a liberal hero; many people considered other perpetrators gross long before they were outed.

After Eric and I broke up, a friend called to check on me.

"Why is it always these people who are so vocal that do these things?" he asked.

"It's like anti-gay people who turn out to be gay themselves," I answered. "Maybe it's because of self-loathing, because they need a mask over who they really are."

Over lunch with another friend, we talked about how Eric's whole platform was as a champion of women.

She said, "Isn't that always the case—those who are most staunch about an issue, whether it be women's rights or being anti-gay, turn out to be hiding something."

The disconnect between Eric's public persona and his private behavior resonated when I watched the documentary *Leaving Neverland*. It was triggering for me to hear Michael Jackson's victims talk about the ways in which they were made to feel that his abuse of them was an expression of love, that they couldn't tell anyone or they'd be dead. Whether the perpetrators are pop stars or priests, they are frequently harbored by their fans and communities because they are perceived as doing good.

I felt this acutely when I read about a pediatrician, Dr. Johnnie Barto, in Johnstown, Pennsylvania, who had sexually abused child patients for decades. He was married, a father of four. He sang in the church choir and served on the school board. In the late 1990s, three families tried to expose him, but he wasn't caught. Instead, the community rallied around him. In April 2000, hundreds gathered at a local restaurant to declare their support for him. He said to this adoring crowd, "I have said before, and I will say again, that my life has been devoted to the welfare of children. I have never, and would never, act in any way to harm a child."

Barto continued to practice for many years, until December 2017, when a twelve-year-old girl described to her mother how he had asked her to sit on his lap while he touched her vaginal area. In January 2018, he was arrested. Pennsylvania attorney general Josh Shapiro made an announcement asking victims to come forward, and a "torrent" of calls started coming in. By July, the number of accusers had risen to sixty-nine. Shapiro said, "Dr. Johnnie Barto used his position of authority—as the pediatrician who families relied on—to feed his own sick desires and take advantage of parents and children seeking basic health care."

In a March 17, 2019, story on NBCNews.com, Erika Brosig, one of Barto's victims from the 1990s, said, "You know how predators groom victims? Well, he groomed a community to believe he could do no wrong."

As my deliberation continued, I wrote a letter to Eric, knowing I would never send it:

> I am recovering from a year+ of abuse by you. I don't expect you to acknowledge what you did. I don't even expect you to be aware of what you did. You were high on alcohol and Ambien much of the time. But a guy who hits me until I agree to do something I will never do, like find a young woman to have a three-

way, or call him master or daddy, that's a sick guy. You are no better than Harvey Weinstein.

I'm not scared of you. Even though you said early on in our relationship that you would have to kill me if we broke up, that you could have my phone tapped and have me followed, I've already faced death, and it doesn't scare me. I can imagine that you would write me off as a crazy person. Well, I'm not. I have a lot of people who care about me privately and who knew about your controlling, demeaning treatment.

I had never been in an abusive relationship before, and I had never been with an alcoholic. Now I know. It's not okay how you treated me. You need help. I hope you get it.

The day after I found out about the previous girlfriend, Jennifer Gonnerman and I spoke again. She wanted me to talk with a lawyer. She knew which one: Roberta "Robbie" Kaplan. She sent me a video of Kaplan speaking about marriage equality, which she had helped make a reality through her representation of LGBTQIA+ activist Edith Windsor in the landmark 2013 Supreme Court case that overturned the Defense of Marriage Act. Jen reached out to Kaplan on my behalf, and we arranged to speak by phone a few days later.

As I described my experiences with Eric to Kaplan, I could hear her making noises as if she were disgusted. I told her I didn't know what I was going to do, but that I would keep her posted.

I called Jennifer Friedman to fill her in. I needed help figuring out the path forward. When I told her about the previous girlfriend, she said, "Now there's you and her. Others must be out there. He's been divorced for twenty years." We talked about the possibility of filing a police report, that over the course of a year this was a pattern of behavior. She asked me to articulate one or two of the most memorable incidents. She said that criminal law gets into minutiae; the assertion had to be tight.

I said I wanted to keep a low profile. She talked about how coming forward and being safe were in conflict. If I chose to come forward, he would come after me publicly. If I didn't come forward, he would move on. But he would abuse his next girlfriend, too. Didn't I want to stop that?

I told her that I didn't see myself coming forward anytime soon. By laying out the abuse I dealt with, I would leave myself open to being abused more by the publicity. However, I wouldn't feel good about myself if I didn't come forward. I knew what my goals would be: warn other women, get him to step down and get help, and open up a conversation about intimate violence.

Friedman had a friend in a New York City district attorney's office. If I wanted an expert opinion, she said, she could speak to that person. If Eric's behavior became known, he would likely be investigated, and everyone would hold Eric's hand until they were told they couldn't. Certainly, some people had heard the rumors, but they were just rumors. What was needed was for his victims to come out with facts.

I worried about widening the net of people who knew. I didn't want to risk the possibility of a journalist being tipped off. I imagined the media storm I would get caught up in. Considering my hesitation to come forward, Friedman and I discussed that for the moment I would simply document everything. Unless I were willing to go to the police, she suggested, it would be unwise to do anything else. Her advice was to stay calm and be careful about whom I talked to.

Shortly after, while in a cab, I saw an ad on the taxi's TV screen: "Reporting a sexual assault to the NYPD could lead to the perpetrator being brought to justice, future assaults being prevented, and connect you with important resources. The choice is yours."

Why didn't I go to the police? I had deep respect and admiration for the police, but I didn't trust the process. I knew people who had had negative experiences with the police when powerful men were involved. In my case, my abuser was the top law enforcement official in New York. If he had any inkling I was talking to the police, I was convinced he would come after me.

Jennifer Friedman suggested I meet with her and her mentor Dorchen Leidholdt, a survivors' rights advocate, to talk through everything. She felt that Leidholdt would provide solid, objective advice. I gave Friedman permission to speak with her about my situation. Friedman later told me that when she explained to Leidholdt that there was a case involving a powerful New York state politician, Leidholdt tried to guess who it was. She named various men until she got to Eric's name, and then it clicked. She thought it must be him. She had worked with Eric on strangulation legislation. She felt the pieces fit together; they made sense. He had put himself out there as such an ally of women.

We arranged to meet at Leidholdt's office, but then I received the address: 120 Broadway. That was the address of Eric's office. My heart dropped. I asked to change the location, and we met at a law firm elsewhere.

After hearing about my experience, Leidholdt said, "He's a sexual sadist." We talked about getting a restraining order. She looked at my correspondence with Eric and noted, in one exchange, that I had phrased carefully that I wanted him to respect my wishes not to communicate. She said that his continuing to reach out to me after such a request could be deemed stalking, which was illegal. But she made clear to me that if I got a restraining order, the cat would be out of the bag before I had the chance to come forward, and he would certainly try to silence me.

During my call with Robbie Kaplan, we had spoken about filing a civil claim, in which case I would get a settlement. But I didn't want the money. I also looked into filing an ethics complaint. A friend knew someone who had worked on ethics issues in the attorney general's office. She trusted this person completely to keep it confidential and said she wouldn't disclose any identifying details. I told her to ask about the procedure. She reported back that she got an answer she couldn't have anticipated: basically, the process of filing an ethics complaint was not guaranteed to be confidential, meaning that Eric might get wind of it before it was dealt with.

Another friend offered to connect me with his longtime friend who had been a top lawyer for New York State but was now in private practice. My friend thought it would be good for me to speak with this man to understand the kind of inquiry that might get initiated if there were stories about Eric being a perpetrator. My friend was sure this person would be willing to talk to me, so he wrote his cell phone number on a blue index card and gave it to me. He told me to wait until he had time to give his friend a heads-up.

My friend called at around 7:00 p.m. that same day. He had spoken with his friend, who was sorry, but he couldn't speak with me. He had worked with Eric before, so there was a conflict of interest, but he could connect me with another lawyer who would be helpful. My heart dropped—another of the many times it had been dropping as revelations and coincidences piled up. I became deeply scared. I felt for the first time that it might get back to Eric what I was contemplating doing. I started shaking as I hung up the phone. A few minutes later, I called my friend back. I wanted reassurance that my story would be safe. My friend said he hadn't given my name. He just told this person that he had a friend who had dated Eric and he had a drinking problem and was bad to her.

Thereafter, I felt scared many times, but I threw myself into my work and spending time with a close circle of friends. In those days after I found out about Eric's previous girlfriend, I was knee-deep in producing content for the *Glamour* Women of the Year Awards. One day, I got together with a designer friend who was loaning me a dress for the ceremony. The first thing he said was, "I'm so sorry about you and Eric."

I asked, "How do you know?" I had told only a handful of people about the breakup.

He said that Eric had reached out to him about having dinner. My friend thought he was going to see both of us, as he usually did, and was surprised when I wasn't there. When he asked Eric how I was doing, Eric told him we had split. Later on in the dinner, Eric asked our friend to introduce him to women because it was hard for him to meet people in the type of work that he did.

I gasped. Eric was going to do to another woman what he

had done to me, and I wanted to stop that from happening. But I still didn't know how.

At the *Glamour* Women of the Year Summit (a day of panels and performances that preceded the awards ceremony), I heard woman after woman on the stage talk about the Me Too movement and the importance of speaking up. Sheila Nevins, then the president of HBO Documentary Films, talked about how the traditional rules of the game were that women slept with their bosses. Cameron Russell, a model, talked about how the highest compliment given to a model was "She'll do anything." When Russell was starting out, she was told she would have trouble getting booked because she was a virgin.

On the way to the awards ceremony that night, I saw a sign on a bus stop for a show called *The Opposition* on Comedy Central. The tagline was "Trust no one." At the event, journalists Megan Twohey and Jodi Kantor of the *New York Times* spoke from the podium about their uncovering of the Weinstein story. A group of survivors that included Aly Raisman, the Olympic gymnast who was part of the Sister Army that had taken down sports doctor Larry Nassar, and Anita Hill took the stage. We all stood and clapped and cried. As the applause continued, Anita Hill looked up and around at the crowd. She lifted her arms slightly, as if she were receiving the praise that she had deserved for decades.

By coincidence, during the dinner afterward I was seated next to Megan Twohey. I expressed my admiration for her. I was keeping a big secret, but I did say to her that there were many powerful perpetrators who needed to be exposed.

She said, "It seems like you have something to get off your chest."

A few weeks after the *Glamour* awards, I told Cindi Leive—the editor in chief of *Glamour*, in whom I had already confided—that I felt I was getting closer to knowing what I wanted to do. I had explored so many legal pathways for stopping Eric's cycle of abuse, but they all seemed connected to him in some way. It was really the court of public opinion that might be my best shot. I told her I was going to Portland for a few weeks, where I would reflect on my decision, and would reconnect with her after I returned.

The day I left for Portland, December 26, there was a feature about Eric in the *New York Times*: "New York's Attorney General in Battle with Trump." My eyes opened wide when I got to this part: "Certainly, Mr. Schneiderman and Mr. Trump have little in common. Mr. Trump watches a lot of TV and craves his McDonald's. Mr. Schneiderman does yoga. 'Other than sports, I really don't watch TV much anymore,' Mr. Schneiderman said." But he watched TV every night, when I was trying to fall asleep.

The month before, Samantha Bee had done a special segment with Eric on her show, *Full Frontal*, that included a cartoon of him as Spiderman, except he was "Schneider-Man." A friend emailed me, "Hi Tanya. Hope all is well! Was watching Samantha Bee last night, and lo and behold there is Schneider-Man. Hilarious, and, as far as politicians go, he is definitely a superhero."

In addition, there had been a profile about Eric in GQ: "New York Attorney General Eric Schneiderman on What It Takes to Keep Trump in Check." The subheader was "a conversation with the man who has been a thorn in the president's side for years." Eric was quoted as saying, "There are always those who will seek to undermine and discredit our work, but as the people's lawyer, you get used to that."

As I made my way to Portland, I thought, "This is what I'm up against."

A few months before I met Eric, in the summer of 2016, an enormous tree fell on my house in Portland. I spend time in Portland in large part because of the trees. They calm me. I can stare at them for hours. They are majestic, prehistoric, and inspiring. I think the trees and nature of Portland contribute to its reputation as a great city for writers. Luckily, this tree damaged only an exterior part of the house. Skilled arborists and contractors put everything back together.

After Eric and I broke up, I was telling a friend about the falling of the tree. She lived in northern California, and her husband was a firefighter who had dealt with some of the biggest wildfires in American history. She believed in the symbolism of trees. She asked me what kind of tree it was. When I said it was a big-leaf maple, she told me it's a tree much revered for its canopy, protection, and sweetness, that its wood is used in wands and charms of protection. She said the tree might have been a) getting my attention and b) offering medicine. She felt my relationship with Eric was like the falling of the tree: a shaking of my foundation, but the house was okay. The damage could be fixed.

Like trees, books often intersect with my life. When I was writing my first book, Sonali Deraniyagala's memoir, *Wave*, appeared. She writes about losing generations of her family— her parents, her children, and her husband—in the December 2004 tsunami in Sri Lanka, and yet she ends the book, stunningly, on a note of hope. On keeping her family alive and close around her even after they were gone, she says: "More and more now I keep my balance while staring into us. And I welcome this, a small triumph. It lights me up." After I read *Wave*, I thought that if she could go on, then I must, too.

As I was deciding whether to come forward, I was reading *When Women Were Birds* by Terry Tempest Williams, who writes, "To withhold words is power. But to share our words with others, openly and honestly, is also power."

When I was in Portland, I treated those weeks like they might be my last on earth. I spent New Year's Eve watching my friends' band Pink Martini play at Schnitzer Hall. I felt huge gratitude for my friends there and everywhere, for my home, for my career. In addition to *Glamour*, I had started collaborating with Planned Parenthood and was in the beginning stages of developing a new campaign that would ultimately be titled "UNSTOPPABLE." The title was inspired by a speech Cecile Richards had given at the first Women's March, in January 2017. She said, "One of us can be dismissed. Two of us can be ignored. But together, we are a movement, and we are unstoppable."

After I returned to New York, I met with Cindi Leive and told her I had made my decision. I was scared, but I was ready to have a conversation with David Remnick. Because of the respect I had for the *New Yorker* and because of its courageous Me Too reporting, I felt that my story would be safe with him. That weekend he and I emailed each other, and we set up a time to speak.

CHAPTER 11

COMING FORWARD

Before I met with Remnick, I let him read my first-person anonymous narrative about my experience. It was about fifteen pages long. I also sent it to a trusted friend whom I had told that I was exploring coming forward. She sent me an email:

> His behavior is even worse and more repulsive than
> I imagined. I am so enraged that he inflicted this on
> you. I'm enraged that he acted like a righteous women's
> advocate when he's so clearly filled with anger toward
> them. The slave talk is shockingly racist. I remember
> early on, when you first told me that he criticized your
> hair and clothes and didn't like you talking on the
> phone—it felt ominous and reminded me of the way
> my stepfather acted toward my mother. I remember
> those times you told me how severe his drinking is,
> and I told you that you seemed subdued in the rela-
> tionship. I wish I would have read between the lines
> earlier. I looked up the signs of a domestic abuser
> after I read this, and so much of it is embodied here.

> I'm so, so sorry that you endured this for a year and so
> proud that you want to protect other women.

But really, how could she or any of my friends have been able to read between the lines as long as I wasn't telling them what was happening?

Remnick spoke to a few friends of mine at the *New Yorker* to get their opinion of me. One of them was Jennifer Gonnerman. She told him that she'd known me for more than twenty years, that she had gone with me to get my things from Eric's place, and that within twenty-four hours she had found someone, a previous girlfriend, who had had a similar experience with him.

When Remnick and I got together at a café, he made it clear that our conversation would be confidential and off the record, that it was preliminary and between us alone. He said that he had read my first-person account and asked me what I wanted to do. I said I didn't know, but if the *New Yorker* were interested in pursuing the story, I would participate. He said that a first-person story was tough, because it was a "he-said, she-said" situation and hard to fact-check unless there were photos or a police report. I told him I didn't have that kind of evidence. Also, although Eric slapped me hard, he never gave me a black eye, and with my dark skin, slap marks were less likely to be visible.

I thought, "Do I need to have gotten a black eye to be believed?"

We agreed that I would be even more careful about telling anyone, and that I would give him time to think about what to do.

This was mid-January. I was still working at the Condé Nast building, One World Trade Center. Soon after I met with Remnick, I saw him in the Condé Nast cafeteria while I was with a friend who worked at the *New Yorker*. Remnick waved, and I waved back, but my friend didn't notice. I didn't know if I was supposed to acknowledge him. I saw him again that same week. Synchronicity is a curious thing. At that point, I'd been going to that dining room for about seven months, but only after I got together with Remnick did I see him there twice in one week.

Soon thereafter, I received an email from Eric: "T, I am trying to get backstage passes to the Grammys on Sunday night, feb 28. Would you like to come as my plus 1? Of all the people I know, it seems right to take you."

When he reached out to me, aside from feeling sick, I had two thoughts:

1) He wasn't seeing anyone, so he wasn't abusing someone else, which I found reassuring.
2) He had no idea what I was thinking.

I hadn't heard from him in a few months, and to hear from him then dragged me back into fear. I felt my insides shake.

I was about to go to Los Angeles to attend the Makers Conference, which celebrates women's stories and achievements. Before I went, I thought about the previous girlfriend I had found out about through Jennifer Gonnerman. I knew she lived in LA. I looked her up online and went to her Twitter page. To my surprise, she was following me. I decided to send her a direct message, simply saying that I was going to be in

LA if she had any time. She wrote back right away with her number. I planned to text her after I arrived.

In LA, I visited Danzy Senna. We hadn't seen each other since she had been in New York to speak at the Brooklyn Book Festival many months before. This time, she told me that she was so freaked out by what I had described to her about Eric that she wrote a record of our conversation and emailed it to herself and her husband. She remembered asking me if I knew of other women he had done this to. Back then, I didn't. She remembered that I had told her Eric was at some New Age retreat and that she wanted to go with me right then and there to get my things from his place. She said that I was one of her oldest friends, and she was worried that something bad would happen to me. She said she kept thinking about Nicole Brown Simpson, O. J.'s murdered wife.

I paused to take this in. Then I told her that I was thinking about coming forward.

She said, "The most important thing is you're out. You're safe and seem better than ever."

A day later, I texted Eric's previous girlfriend, and we arranged to meet at a café. I arrived first and sat at a table in the back.

When she got there, she asked, "Is this okay for you?"

I responded, "Is it for you?"

She said it felt like we were on display, so we walked out. We walked through a parking lot to a bench at the edge that looked out over a lower parking lot.

The stories poured out of her. She shared my sense that when he first slapped her during sex, it was as if he were testing her out. From there, the abuse escalated. He would hold up her leg admiringly and then say she had thick ankles. He would touch her eyes, stretch out the skin around them, and say she needed Botox. He asked her to find women for three-ways. When she confronted him about his treatment of her, he said that she wasn't sexually liberated and that she was depriving him of his needs. She described him as a master of psychological manipulation. She talked about the meditators he surrounded himself with. She thought they were all shams. She wanted him to see a therapist with her. He found one, whom he paid under the table, and the therapist told her she was overreacting.

At one point I looked for my phone to check the time. She looked worried and asked if I was recording our conversation. I said no. She wondered if anyone was surveilling us. I found it striking that she felt this level of fear so long after her involvement with Eric had ended. I reassured her that we were alone. She began again: "He toyed with my heart."

She said he tried to position himself as a good guy and someone who cared. He was politically liberal and attractive.

"The optics of it looked so good." She might become Mrs. Schneiderman, she thought.

She said she lost a lot of weight. She knew that if she stayed, she would become a skeleton of herself. Of the end, she said, "I'd had enough."

I felt as if I were hearing her tell my story, except it was hers.

After they broke up, she told a few people about her experience with him. She told people in political circles. She said there were definitely rumors going around about Eric's behavior. She had been approached a few times by reporters, and she had considered exposing him but was scared. Some people told her to keep quiet. Instead, she wrote out her account and put it in a safe-deposit box in case anything happened to her. She gave the key to two friends. She felt that she had been silenced by fear, and she had felt alone. At the time, she treaded softly. She said that to this day she hadn't been able to open her heart to anyone. She said she wanted her self back. She said times had changed—referring to Me Too.

A few years before, she had heard through a friend about a woman who had dated Eric and talked about him slapping her around. The woman had abruptly ended the relationship. I told her that in abusing me, Eric had messed with the wrong woman. I told her I was thinking about coming forward. She didn't know if she would be able to join me, but she told me she would say, "I believe Tanya one hundred percent."

The time had come for me to go to the Makers Conference. We hugged and parted ways. Later, when we spoke on the phone, she said that normally after talking about him, she felt fear, but not after talking to me. She also said, "I feel protective of you."

I began to feel that I had to come forward, not only for the women who might date him after me but for this woman, too.

She told me, "In you is a bit of a savior. You are the answer to a question."

I wasn't sure how to respond. I didn't want to make too much of the part I was about to play.

The theme of the Makers Conference was "Raise Your Voice." I heard woman after woman talk about the changing times. I listened to Marcia Clark, the prosecutor in the O. J. Simpson trial, speak and thought about Danzy's mentioning

Nicole Brown Simpson. I went to a talk by Gloria Steinem and Amy Richards at which Richards said that the Simpson trial was the moment when people first heard about domestic violence in a very public way.

Everywhere I turned at the conference was a story of abuse. One speaker said that victims needed to know that if they spoke out, there would be no retaliation against them. But I thought to myself, as I often did, "What do you do if your abuser is the top law enforcement official in your state?"

TIME'S UP had recently begun, and many of the women involved in it participated in the conference. In the audience was Robbie Kaplan, the lawyer with whom I had spoken on the phone a few months before. She had become the cofounder of the TIME'S UP Legal Defense Fund. Amy Richards introduced us. Kaplan and I simply said hi and made no allusions to our previous conversation.

Around then, I had a dream about trying to hide my first-person narrative from Eric. I was still with him, but I had hidden the hard copy in a backpack at the back of a closet. He returned home. He was like a child. He wanted me to take care of him. He wanted me to have sex with him. I didn't want to, but I also felt like doing it would make him less likely to find my essay. While he went to the bathroom, I worried that he might open the closet. I rushed to take the piece out of the backpack and tried to figure out where to put it. Then, suddenly, I was not in his apartment but in a house with many levels. It was a very narrow building. I opened an exit door, and there were no stairs, just a slope. I slid all the way from the top of the house to the ground floor.

When I woke, I opened a news app on my phone and saw

Eric's face. His photo was the thumbnail for an article on *Politico* about Democratic attorneys general. It cited him as aspiring to be governor of New York.

I was preparing to leave for Sri Lanka that day when the Rob Porter story broke, about how he, the White House staff secretary, had a pattern of abusing his intimate partners. Jennie Willoughby, his ex-wife, described him as "a man who could be both charming and romantic and fun—and even thoughtful and kind; and horribly angry and manipulative." The White House had known about the allegations as early as January 2017 but had allowed Porter to keep his job. Dahlia Lithwick wrote a piece for *Slate* titled "Rob Porter's History of Domestic Abuse Wasn't a Secret. It's Just That No One Cared." Senator Orrin Hatch had previously called the women "character assassins," but after the story became public, he issued a statement:

> I am heartbroken by today's allegations. In every
> interaction I've had with Rob, he has been courteous,
> professional, and respectful. My staff loved him and
> he was a trusted advisor. I do not know the details of
> Rob's personal life. Domestic violence in any form is
> abhorrent. I am praying for Rob and those involved.

I received a few texts, including from Jennifer Friedman, wanting to know how I was doing. They were worried about how the news would affect me, but I felt a strengthening. I felt a door opening. Against the backdrop of Me Too, the press was finally talking about domestic violence. Lithwick cited Catharine MacKinnon's op-ed about Me Too for the *New York Times*:

It typically took three to four women testifying that they had been violated by the same man in the same way to even begin to make a dent in his denial. That made a woman, for credibility purposes, one-fourth of a person . . . Even when she was believed, nothing he did to her mattered as much as what would be done to him if his actions against her were taken seriously. His value outweighed her sexualized worthlessness.

Willoughby, Porter's ex-wife, wrote an essay for *Time*, in which she called out the president, who had defended Porter:

The words "mere allegation" and "falsely accused" [are] meant to imply that I am a liar. That Colbie Holderness is a liar. That the work Rob was doing in the White House was of higher value than our mental, emotional or physical wellbeing. That his professional contributions are worth more than the truth. That abuse is something to be questioned and doubted . . . Thankfully, my strength and worth are not dependent on outside belief—the truth exists whether the President accepts it or not.

She ended her piece with a message to others in abusive situations: "It is real. You are not crazy. You are not alone. I believe you."

I knew that coming forward publicly would be my best chance at effecting change. I also recognized the possibility in my story for increased public awareness and education around intimate violence. If Eric weren't an important, powerful man, no one would care.

Soon after I arrived in Sri Lanka, my grandmother—my mother's mother—asked a lot of questions about Eric, whom she mistakenly called "Ned."

"What happened?"

I responded, "He was controlling."

"You used to like him."

"But then he started to be more controlling. He wanted me to dress a certain way, do my hair a certain way. I couldn't be free."

Suddenly she asked, about my father, "Did he hit Mummy?"

"Yes."

"Often?"

"Yes."

"Did you see it?"

"Yes. He was Jekyll and Hyde."

"And Ned, was he also Jekyll and Hyde?"

"Yes."

She asked if he hit me. We just stared at each other.

She said, "At that time, I was happy for you. But then you found you had a big frog."

She told me she was tired and wanted to sleep. I went downstairs to my bedroom and opened my computer to find that an email had come in from Eric: "Sorry to bother you. But I need to speak with you about a sensitive matter. When is a good time to speak?"

I wrote simply that I was traveling and with my family.

He wrote again—trying, I felt, to get me agitated into feeling that I had to talk to him right away: "This will be brief, but is time sensitive if you have 3 minutes for a telephone call. I would not bother you if it was not important."

I started shaking, feeling those rapid palpitations of my heart that I had come to recognize so well. Context is as important as or more important than content. The timing of when Eric reached out to me spoke volumes. He'd been playing the game of what he said he was like, keeping up appearances. But the seams were beginning to rip.

Aside from the Rob Porter story, it was all over the news about Eric filing a lawsuit against the Weinstein Company and blocking its sale. Many leading figures in the Me Too and TIME'S UP movements thanked him publicly. Actress Annabella Sciorra, who had broken her silence about being repeatedly raped by Weinstein, tweeted praise for Eric's lawsuit. Actress Jessica Chastain "liked" Sciorra's tweet. Eric was positioning himself as their hero. Journalist Andrew Ross Sorkin explained in the *New York Times* that when Eric held a news conference about the case, "He spoke at a lectern with the words 'Justice for Victims' written across it."

Eric appeared on PBS's *Frontline* to talk about how he was holding Weinstein accountable. To me, he seemed to have a Weinstein-level pathology, as if he were purposely provoking a media person to dig. Around that time, Eric spoke at an event called "Fight Back Like a Girl," hosted by the women's health nonprofit Lady Parts Justice and political organizing platform #VOTEPROCHOICE. When the *New Yorker* and the *New York Times* shared the Pulitzer Prize for Public Service for their Me Too reporting in April, Eric tweeted: "Without the reporting of the @nytimes and the @newyorker—and the brave women and men who spoke up about the sexual harassment they endured at the hands of powerful men—there would not be the critical national reckoning underway. A well-deserved honor."

I thought, "He's writing the story for me."

While I was in Sri Lanka, I didn't tell anyone in my family what was happening, that I had been in an abusive relationship and was thinking of coming forward. I felt that if I told one person, the whole family would find out. And if that happened, then all of Sri Lanka would know.

I thought about a friend who recalled, after Eric and I broke up, my telling her about his not letting me eat meat in front of him and how he wanted me in his apartment but wouldn't come to mine. She said that type of controlling behavior of a woman in her forties was not normal. Before I left Sri Lanka, my aunt, who had cooked a lavish spread to welcome Eric when he was with me the year before, pulled me aside. She put her arm around me and whispered, "Now you can eat chicken."

On the plane back from Sri Lanka, it hit me how far away I had gotten from everything in America and how close I could be to having my privacy and life ruined for some time. After I returned to New York, David Remnick and I spoke, and he told me that he had decided to assign a reporter to the story. At the moment, she was working on a big piece, so he would speak with her after she had turned it in.

He said, "You know a lot of people. Don't tell anyone about this."

This was going to be the scariest thing I had ever done. I had been in Sri Lanka during curfews and bomb threats. I had gotten on a plane a few days after 9/11. I had dealt with cancer. But this was different. This involved putting out intimate details about myself. I felt embarrassed and ashamed that my sex life would be exposed and that people might see that before they saw me. I valued my freedom, my ability to escape and be unbothered. I wished that I could come forward without my name being disclosed. I vacillated between wanting to hide and go underground and wanting to go public and make sure this never happened to anyone else.

I considered moving. I loved my building, but it was hard to hide there. With a central courtyard flanked by entryways all around, it was a fishbowl where everyone could see my comings and goings. I went and looked at a few apartments. Meanwhile, I tried to go about my business as usual. I participated in a panel at the Athena Film Festival at Barnard College. I decided to walk home as much of the way as possible. For the first time since I had gotten my things from Eric's place, I was on the Upper West Side. I considered walking toward the area near his building, to conquer my fear. But I felt sick. In New York City, I couldn't get away from the feeling of being sick. I wondered if I should get out of town and stay out of town.

In early March, Remnick and I spoke again, and he told me the reporter would be Jane Mayer. Her other story would be running soon. The second week of March, her explosive piece about the Steele dossier (which contained allegations of misconduct and conspiracy between Trump and Russia) came out. On March 19, she sent me an email to set up a time to talk. We arranged to speak the next day.

That night, I went to a small birthday dinner that Amy Richards was hosting for me. The guests were a group of people who knew what I was dealing with. I felt like it was my last supper. I gave a toast and said that birthdays were not simply markers of being a year older but markers of knowing people longer, and that friends made my world go 'round.

On March 20, my actual birthday, I spoke with Mayer,

with Robbie Kaplan (who was now officially my lawyer) on the call, too. I told Mayer, "I am honored, grateful, and nervous to be talking to you." She had cowritten the book *Strange Justice*, about Anita Hill and Clarence Thomas. She had written *Dark Money*, the book about the Koch brothers that was prominently displayed in Eric's apartment.

I described my experience to her as I had done with Robbie, as I had done with Remnick. As I got to the end, I told her, "He's going to try to kill me or have someone try to kill me."

She said, "He won't kill you. Well, I think if we get three women to talk on the record, he's over. Robbie, don't you think so?"

Robbie responded, "I think you're right."

Later that day, I left for Portland. After I settled into my house, I tried to open a box that had been delivered. The knife I was using slipped and pierced the skin between my thumb and index finger. I started bleeding profusely. I rinsed the wound and applied multiple bandages. When I woke up the next morning, it was still bleeding. I went to the emergency room. The doctor told me I was lucky I hadn't hit a nerve or tendon. As my hand healed, I kept reminding myself to stay grounded in my actions and aware of my surroundings.

Over the next few days, I continued to have conversations with Mayer. During one, she asked, "Why does the public need to know this?"

I answered, "He holds himself out as a feminist and the highest legal authority on equality in the state."

She said, "Yes, it's relevant to voters to know if he really is. But JFK turned out not to be a great guy."

While running errands, I noticed an AT&T store and spontaneously stopped in. I asked the salesperson about a nontraceable phone. I told her I was producing a project that contained sensitive information.

She said, "Like a throwaway phone?"

"Yes."

"We have a lot of women who come in and need phones that aren't attached to their name and number."

I wondered what kind of work these women did. Were they drug dealers or spies?

While she was setting up the phone for me, another salesperson, who had heard me reference my work making movies, talked about how he wanted to be an actor but didn't want to risk moving to Hollywood. He liked having a roof over his head. He liked the outdoors.

It was a perfect sunny day.

After an hour and a half, I was still there. They were having technical difficulties creating my account. We joked about making a documentary called *System Failure*.

When the process was finally complete, the supervisor apologized and said to me, "Happy Easter."

I asked if she needed anything else.

She said, "I just need you to be happy for me the rest of the night. You take care always."

I began to feel like the time had come to prepare important people in my life for the story to come out. I had lunch with a friend and asked, "Am I doing the right thing?"

She said, "You know in your heart of hearts you are. You don't have a choice."

I called Carrie Mae Weems to let her know. Carrie had been present at the beginning and during so many pivotal points in the relationship.

She said, "I'm scared for you. You have a home at my place."

She asked, "Have you heard from Knucklehead?"

I said I had received a few emails from him insisting that we talk.

She said, "I don't know whom to trust." She was horrified by Eric's speaking out against Weinstein, knowing what Eric had done to me and other women.

I called another friend. She was concerned that if my story became public, I wouldn't be able to control the narrative. She encouraged me not to go by the playbook that everyone else had been using with stories of abuse; she wondered if it would be better to take the mic myself and say, "This is what happened to me." She said I could tell the story the way I wanted to tell it. I could do it in a video or another creative way. She said it was an incredibly important and powerful story, but that I should be prepared for a libel suit, that I should marshal a support group of her and other friends.

I called my brother and sister-in-law. My brother really didn't want me to be on the record. He said, "You might not be happy with having been on the record after it comes out. So many women's lives are ruined after they out an abuser." But they both said that they supported me and offered a hiding place in their house.

I spoke with my mother. "I want to talk to you about something. It's not an easy conversation to have."

I described in as little detail as possible how Eric had slapped me, belittled me, and tried to control me. After I finished, she sounded weirdly relieved. "I thought you were going to tell me the cancer had come back, and *that* I wouldn't have been able to take."

She started talking about my father. She said that when he was dying from lung cancer, "Daddy told your uncle he was suffering because of what he did to me." She went on about my father, "I hate him. I hate him." A few seconds later: "I don't hate him. I sometimes feel . . . I'm glad he's dead and gone. I had twenty-four years of suffering. Now twenty-four years since he died. After seeing what happened to me, you should have left after the first time."

I said, "I know, and now I know forever." After a pause, I said, "When it started happening, it was jarring and scary. I thought it was specific to me. I thought he was having a breakdown."

"He will get what's coming to him. You don't have to do it." She meant I didn't have to participate in the story.

I said, "He's been getting away with it for a long time. And he will continue to, unless I do something."

She said she didn't want me to come forward. "I don't want publicity."

I said, "I need support."

This conversation was one of the most candid my mother and I had ever had with each other. I felt a huge sense of relief that I wasn't keeping this secret from her anymore. I felt that she had heard me about needing support.

But a few hours later, she called again. "You should never have stayed with him after the first time. He thought he was a big shot. It's your mistake for not walking. When I see him, I will spit on his face. Because he's the attorney general, people kowtow to him. He thought he's a big deal. We're a bigger deal."

I recognized that my experience was triggering for her, and she was acting out her fears, her past experiences with my father, the inability of many in her family to accept her truth. In the meantime, I was standing by while Jane Mayer conducted her investigation.

CHAPTER 12

THE ROLLER COASTER

I told myself every day, "Don't be afraid. Don't be impatient." In less than two weeks after I first spoke with Jane Mayer, she connected with other ex-girlfriends of Eric's and listened to their stories, which were strikingly similar to mine. She had the material she needed to build a piece, and she wanted to publish it as soon as possible. I told her I needed time to get my life together. I needed to get back to New York and make plans for my security and escape. I knew that without my participation, there would be no story. I knew I held the cards. But I also felt terrible telling Mayer that no, I wasn't ready for the story to be public yet. I emailed her that I needed a week.

She tried to reach me by phone many times, and when she eventually did, she said, "Are you sure you need to worry this much? It's not that difficult to stay safe. I've covered two wars—you can do this." But I told her I couldn't return to New York into a maelstrom. I asked her to give me time.

Although I had no children, I worried about the impact coming forward would have on my extended family and, more so, on my career and reputation. Once I put my story out there,

I wouldn't be able to take it back, and I couldn't anticipate how my life would change. I kept reminding myself that my friends and my work were solid and would still be there for me. A few people might drift away, and that would be okay. I had a handful of friends who had told me not to do anything, but they were far outnumbered by those who told me that I knew what I had to do. I felt that if I spoke my truth, then others would be able to, too. I hoped that by coming forward I could pave the way for the women who were abused before me finally to speak their truths as well. When the history of Me Too would be written, I wouldn't be able to live with being the one who was too scared to protect other women. The news cycle would pass, and then no one would care anymore. In a few years, no one might remember Eric's name. I didn't expect him ever to acknowledge the harm he did to me, the ways in which he eroded my self-esteem. I had to fight against my own disappointment that the women before me could have prevented him from doing this to me. It became clear during the reporting of the story that previous girlfriends had told themselves to stay silent, or had people telling them not to do anything.

I spoke with a friend who taught at a university that was dealing with its own reckoning over a professor who had harassed colleagues and students. She talked about how Eric was a high-profile guy with many opportunities to meet women. She encouraged me to go on the record in order to minimize the access he had to women he could then abuse. She said the story was becoming a many-headed monster, and not every part would turn out how I wanted it to, but she agreed that I would be doing the right thing.

When *Time* magazine named "The Silence Breakers" its

2017 Person of the Year, it conducted an online poll that showed "eighty-two percent of respondents said women are more likely to speak out about harassment since the Weinstein allegations." Eighty-five percent said that they "believe the women making allegations of sexual harassment."

In early April, a woman testified under oath that Eric Greitens, then the governor of Missouri, had sexually coerced and abused her. Pressure mounted for him to resign. Around that time, I received an email from Eric. Because I wasn't responding to him, he replied twice to his own email, increasing the urgency. The tone felt similar to that of the emails he had sent while I was in Sri Lanka, insisting we had to talk, then becoming angry that I wouldn't.

He wrote, "I thought we parted with a high degree of mutual respect, but I guess I was wrong." In his next email, he claimed he had to talk to me about Weinstein. He wanted to know if Weinstein had donated money to the films I was producing around the election. In 2016, Eric had in fact mentioned to Weinstein the work I was producing, and Weinstein had said he wanted to support it. But he had never donated to it. To stop the email train, I responded with a simple "no."

I showed the emails to Jennifer Friedman. She said Eric kept showing his true colors, which she found weirdly reassuring. "You don't even have to push him that hard. He's totally clueless and lacks self-awareness. A normal person would say, 'Hey, is something wrong?' They wouldn't lash out. They would be concerned."

When I was back in New York, I was able to focus on preparing for the day the story came out. Amy Richards strongly suggested I get security training. She connected me with Gavin de Becker's team. They counseled me on my safety and provided me with recommendations.

At some point before the story came out, Eric would find out about it. I felt the gravity of the risk I would be taking. I thought about the many women who had been sharing their Me Too stories and wondered what precautions they had taken to safeguard their security.

Among the first precautions I took was to remove my name from the buzzer list and my mailbox at my building. I also deleted my social media accounts; the social media life was never for me anyway. Shortly before my first book came out, my publicist encouraged me to join all platforms, but it never felt quite right. It was wonderful reconnecting with friends from college, high school, and even elementary school. Other than that, I didn't need social media. After I deleted my accounts, I was more curious about people because I didn't already know what they were up to. I liked them more because I wasn't being constantly updated on the mundane details of their lives.

On April 25, I met Jane Mayer for dinner in my neighborhood on the Lower East Side. We spent about three hours together. I found her easy to talk to, but I kept reminding myself that she wasn't my friend. It's the skill of the best reporters to be likeable and make the subject feel liked by them. At one point, I told her, "I wish my name didn't have to be mentioned." But I submitted myself to the process of journalism.

She asked if I would be amenable to allowing the article to include the photo of a bruised Eric in the hospital the day before the president's inauguration. I said I needed to think about it. I knew that I was fine with the photo being described, but I wasn't comfortable with it being shown. I felt it would be all over the tabloids in a second. I had straightforward objectives that didn't require extreme measures to be achieved; the similar stories from women being interviewed independently of one another were enough. But I had the image in my phone, so I did decide to let her see it.

The next day, Mayer and I met at Robbie Kaplan's office, where we were joined by Ronan Farrow, who had recently been added as a reporter on the investigation. He and Mayer had not collaborated before, but correspondence with the multiple women involved was proving unwieldy, and Farrow was helping with that. He also had leads on other women with similar stories.

Mayer and Farrow had me tell my story from beginning to end, and they occasionally asked questions. I remember being struck by their calm composure, gentle listening, and clear reasoning. I felt like I was in the best possible hands, and that the outcome was now out of my hands. This story must come out. It had taken Farrow a year to get women on the record about Weinstein. With this case, it had taken a matter of weeks.

As we walked out of the office, Farrow thanked me. He also said, "You might want to turn off your phone for a while when this comes out."

Afterward, while I was at a work meeting, four breaking news alerts popped up on my phone. Bill Cosby had been convicted.

I said to those in the meeting, "That would not have happened a year ago."

My story, I knew, could drop any day. The question was: with which women participating? First there was me, then there had been three, then there were two, now there might be four. Would Mayer and Farrow hear back from a fifth? The number was going up and down and all around in those final days.

And then there was a leak. To the *New York Times*. A reporter there was trying to reach other previous girlfriends. About a week later, the reporter emailed Robbie Kaplan, and then called her with a tactless message that she'd heard that Robbie had a client with a Me Too story about Eric Schneiderman.

I wrote to Robbie, "She's got no story if no one talks to her."

I decided I didn't need to hide yet, but I wanted to escape my thoughts, so I went gallery-hopping. I visited Hank Willis Thomas's exhibition *What We Ask Is Simple*, in which he depicted historical images of protests and the civil rights movement. In one piece, a sign read, "Men of quality are not threatened by women for equality."

The Tribeca Film Festival was on, and I went to a screening of *RX: Early Detection—A Cancer Journey with Sandra Lee* and the reception afterward. Governor Andrew Cuomo was there to support his partner Sandra Lee's premiere. I was overwhelmed by the secret I was keeping inside. I couldn't help but think that Cuomo knew what was brewing with regard to Eric.

I hadn't eaten. I had a bourbon. It went to my head. I went home. As I walked toward the entryway of my building, I lost my footing and fell. It's embarrassing to fall down in public, to lose one's step with others' eyes watching.

I started to anticipate the fallout and various scenarios after Mayer and Farrow's story came out. The race the *New York Times* reporter was now imposing would accelerate the story's release. I thought it would be Eric's word against mine.

He would say that he remembered things differently. Memory and experience can be subjective. There are often two realities, the victim's and the abuser's, but one is telling the truth and one is trying to squash it. In this case, where multiple women very different from one another and interviewed independently were telling similar stories, I felt objectivity would emerge.

It wasn't just the exposing of this story that frightened me, but also the scrutiny of me and my personal life. When people met me, that story might be the first thing they connected with me. When they googled me, it might be the result they noticed most. I expected these reactions: "She's being an opportunist." "She stayed with him." "She didn't tell anyone about the physical abuse for a long time, so how do we know it was real?" Some people would judge me; some would doubt me; some would have my back. But, ultimately, this wasn't about me. It was about the women who wouldn't be abused by him in the future.

The next day I went to the premiere of the television miniseries *The Fourth Estate* by Liz Garbus. Because the series was about the *New York Times*, I was in a room crawling with reporters, many of whom I knew. I was keeping a big secret from all of them. I felt the bomb ticking.

Yet another reporter from the *Times* reached out to Robbie Kaplan directly. Robbie told her she couldn't talk about it. The reporter then texted her: "Robbie, that thing we discussed the other night is on my mind. What's eating at me, reportorially, is that this is the guy charged with investigating [New York County district attorney Cyrus] Vance (not to mention so many others). If there's a problematic pattern there, it's got to be publicly documented. Is the issue that the women are reluctant to see this reported?"

I wrote to Robbie, "We have it under control with two of the most trusted journalists in the world." I thought, "What is the *Times* doing, trying to scoop the *New Yorker*?"

The next morning, while I was in a meeting, my phone rang. The screen showed the name of a friend who worked at the *Times*, so I answered.

I said, "I'm in a meeting. Can I call you back in about an hour?"

The voice said, "I think you think I'm someone else."

"Who is this?"

"It's X from the *Times*."

She was the same reporter who had reached out to Robbie. I told her I was in a meeting.

She asked, "Is there a time that's good for—?"

I hung up before she could finish the question.

She tried me repeatedly during the day. I blocked her, both her cell and the *Times* number.

She then sent me an email: "I'd love to chat with you about some of your women's rights activism, when you have a few minutes."

I thought, "Well, that's hilarious."

I forwarded the email to Jane Mayer, who wrote, "They now have your name and are coming up with a bogus excuse to try to pull you in."

The next day, a friend texted that the *Times* reporter had reached out to her wanting to talk about me. She tried to call another friend four times; yet another friend said she had called his office and then his cell. It seemed almost random whom the reporter was contacting. Maybe she was going through my website and contacting people mentioned on it? I alerted those who had any knowledge about what I was dealing with to ignore her and block her number.

One friend called, sounding worried. "Are you in danger?"

I said, "I'll be okay."

It actually entertained me, the woman's fumbling around, trying to scoop the story. The reporter didn't seem to understand victims and trauma. You don't lie to or stalk a victim. I thought, "Don't they realize you don't get a Me Too story by harassing the victims?"

A few days later, I spoke with Mayer. She had gotten an email from Eric's PR guy and spoken with him. He said he had heard she was asking questions about Eric. He had heard she was working on a Me Too story. He asked her to let him know.

She simply responded, "Yes. I'll let you know if there's a story."

She said to me wryly, "It's a hot potato."

After I hung up, I worried that Eric now had time to gather his troops and assemble his surrogates. We had lost the advantage of surprise.

I thought, "I'm a nobody. He and his people will try to crush me."

I became more scared. I had worked so hard to keep my story airtight, but one whisper had become a thousand. That weekend, Carrie Mae Weems stayed with me. She said, "Our place in the world is that we should be attractive to men. And we stay silent."

I asked, "Am I doing the right thing?"

"Yes, unfortunately."

Remnick gave me a heads-up that a fact-checker would be calling me, that the story would be coming out soon. I had made plans to leave the country on May 9, but he couldn't guarantee it would run after I was safely gone. We talked about how it had been a roller coaster. I told him I was very scared, shaking all the time, though nobody could tell. He thanked me for my steadfastness, patience, and trust.

That night, I had a dream. I was at One World Trade Center, in the *New Yorker* offices. I was meeting with various people who were prepping for the release of the story. The last I had heard, there were two women on the record, one anonymous and one as background. I was disappointed that more women wouldn't participate. In the dream, a fact-checker from the *New Yorker* called me to say, "Ma'am, be careful as you walk home."

I asked, "Did he deny what was in the story?"

The fact-checker quietly said, "Yes."

"Did he deny that he called me his slave and property?"

"Yes."

"Did he deny that he hit me in bed?"

"Yes."

Then I saw text messages streaming through on my phone. I realized that the story had hit. As I woke up from the dream, my heart was pounding in my ears.

In my waking life, I packed a suitcase, and my friend Julia picked me up and helped me move my things to my friend Catherine's place, where I would hide out until I could leave the country.

On Monday, May 7, Remnick called to say the *New Yorker* was about to contact Eric's office for comment. He said that Eric would then know I was participating.

Remnick said the story made him feel sick, on the one

hand, but confident on the other. He said, "Do I love publishing things like this? It's necessary."

Mayer forwarded me the responses from Eric's office. He was denying most of the allegations, and some of the abuse he claimed was consensual.

Remnick told me, "We're off to the races."

CHAPTER 13

THE FALLOUT

A little before 7:00 p.m. on May 7, I received a text from David Remnick: "The story is up."

I was at a benefit dinner hosted by artist Laurie Anderson and writer A. M. Homes to support Yaddo, the artist residency in Saratoga Springs, New York. I took Laurie aside and told her that I thought I had to leave. She asked why.

I said, "A story just came out."

"Are you in it?"

"Yes."

She said, "Then you've done what you need to do. Don't go."

I stayed. For the next two hours, my phone was blowing up with text messages and missed calls from friends. At the dinner, no one knew what was going on. It was an artsy crowd, and they weren't looking at their phones.

I was there with Julia, so I felt as calm as could be possible. We left a little before the end of dinner. As we walked out to the street, I felt as if I were in an episode of *The Walking Dead*. The streets were quiet. Catherine, with whom I was staying, called to check on me. Her mother, Aggie, was with her and wanted to speak with me. Aggie wanted me to know how sorry she was for me. They were finishing up dinner at a restaurant in the Meatpacking District, a few blocks from where we were. Aggie said to come over so she could give me a hug. Julia and I walked over to the restaurant. Even though the news was everywhere, I felt anonymous and strode over to their table. Aggie and Catherine hugged me, and then Aggie gave us a ride to Catherine's place. Catherine, Julia, and I sat around the dining table. They were tracking the news. I hadn't even read the story yet.

I heard that many New York politicians were calling for Eric to resign. I felt ambivalent about many of these pronouncements. Most didn't express sympathy for the victims. It was all politics, and politics was theater. There were the statements they made, and then there were the truths they themselves had known and hidden.

A breaking news alert came on my phone. Eric had issued a statement:

> In the last several hours, serious allegations, which I strongly contest, have been made against me. While these allegations are unrelated to my professional conduct or the operations of the office, they will effectively prevent me from leading the office's work at this critical time. I therefore resign my office, effective at the close of business on May 8, 2018.

It had been less than three hours since the *New Yorker* story had run. Remnick told me that the outcome was unprecedented. I felt it was a testament to Mayer and Farrow's airtight reporting. The story had landed like a surgical strike.

Eric's ex-wife issued a statement:

> I've known Eric for nearly 35 years as a husband, father and friend. These allegations are completely inconsistent with the man I know, who has always been someone of the highest character, outstanding values and a loving father. I find it impossible to believe these allegations are true.

When I read that, I thought, well, she must have known about his problems—at least based on what I had heard from the previous girlfriend, whom I had connected with a few months before.

Robbie Kaplan emailed to check on me. I called her and said I was with friends, not reading the news.

She said, "Good. You are a hero."

Robbie had always been so matter-of-fact with me that I was surprised and moved by her compliment.

Catherine was receiving calls from mutual friends to check on me. I was feeling less shell-shocked and better able to communicate with people beyond her and Julia. We put the callers on speaker phone. One friend talked about the strange convergence of my story with the Me Too moment. Another was with a group of lawyers in DC who were talking about how the fact that Eric had resigned within a few hours meant the allegations had to be true. She said he needed to enter rehab and be gone.

I spoke with Jennifer Gonnerman, who said that with any piece not as strong as this one, I could have been left twisting in the wind for months. Really, there was nothing to celebrate. It wasn't like I was going to have champagne with friends and toast the outcome. But she said this was one of the first times in history where things hadn't gone wrong for the victims.

Cindi Leive texted that I could read the story and not be ashamed. So, I finally did. As I did, I felt as if I were watching a movie of my life.

I started hearing about the backlash, but it all seemed dumb. On Twitter, a nutjob conspiracy theorist, who had acquired a large following because, like the president, she said crazy untrue things, declared me a "Putin plant." The lamest was probably Trump's counselor Kellyanne Conway, who tweeted, "Gotcha."

I had my computer in front of me and Julia and Catherine by my side. As I read an email that came in, Julia noticed sadness in my expression. I showed her the note. My mother had written to tell me to stop going after "cheap publicity." Julia and Catherine looked sad on my behalf. I had gotten so used to being blamed and criticized by my mother that I had been kind of expecting this reaction. She couldn't put herself in my shoes and see the bigger picture. I had done the right thing.

I also received a note from a relative, advising me to "avoid saying anything further to anyone," like going on talk shows. She also wrote that if I did, I "[might] lose the support of some" who believed I was courageous to come forward.

I was in fact receiving dozens of media requests; I was being offered "platforms" by television talk shows. I knew that the bookers and producers were just doing their jobs, but I felt that this was not a time to gloat. I had already planned not to do any follow-up press; the story would speak for itself.

Eric had stepped down; women had been warned. An unexpected development was that Barbara Underwood was appointed acting attorney general, the first woman to hold the position. I felt comforted. Journalist Rebecca Traister later wrote, "One day in June 2018, I turned on the television and saw Christiane Amanpour, the woman hired to host Charlie Rose's PBS show, interviewing Barbara Underwood, the woman who replaced Eric Schneiderman as New York's attorney general, about a lawsuit she'd just filed against the Trump Foundation." Visible change was taking place.

With regard to my mother and my relative, I had to forgive them or else I would have made myself sick. People can be scared to speak their truths because family members silence them. But then the news exploded in Sri Lanka; it was on the front page of every paper, with some articles focusing salaciously on the "brown slave" terminology. Horrible people, mostly women with too much time and spite on their hands, seized upon the story. Tongues started wagging and stinging, and in Sri Lanka, gossip can kill. My mother was affected by the negativity. However, I felt that anyone who was going to judge me was not someone I needed in my life and not someone my mother should have in her life, either.

Meanwhile, I had been receiving an incredible outpouring of support from friends and strangers all over the world, and I did hear from a few family members, especially among my generation, who applauded my courage and offered me refuge.

The next day, I heard from a friend in my apartment building that a reporter had shown up at my door and slipped a note under it and that an FBI agent had tried to open the door and then slipped a business card under it with a note saying she'd like to talk to me. But I was sequestered at Catherine's. Catherine told me a story about Philippe Petit, who was famous for walking a high-wire between the former Twin Towers of the World Trade Center. He had talked about the importance of staying balanced in order to live longer. He advised putting on one's socks and shoes while standing up. I tried to do so and felt wobbly.

I was worried that my career would be impacted by the *New Yorker* piece. But my boss-to-be at a new arts center called to check on me. He said, "We're still on." Planned Parenthood, for which I had already been working, sent flowers.

The jockeying for Eric's job began almost immediately, with New York City public advocate Letitia James and law professor Zephyr Teachout throwing their hats into the ring. They made public statements denouncing Eric but didn't mention concern for his victims. Meanwhile, the story was being spun through angle after angle. Jane Mayer appeared on WNYC public radio; Ronan Farrow on CNN. I stayed in my cocoon at Catherine's place. The story seemed to have blown up assumptions about intimate violence and domestic violence. It provided a teachable moment. Journalists were writing about consent, abuse, and even racial dynamics in intimate partner relationships.

The Cut ran a feature on "Eric Schneiderman and Men Who Excuse Violence as 'Kink.'" It also ran an informative guide: "Here's How Consent and BDSM Role-Play Actually Work." The sex educator cited in the piece, Barbara Carrellas, took offense at Eric's defense of his actions: "Role play means two people had a conversation and decided: *I think this sounds really hot, now how can we sensibly play this out.*" She said the slapping described in the *New Yorker* article was "bang-on brute violence." According to Carrellas:

> In BDSM role-play face-slapping is a trigger for a whole lot of people. The trigger level is so high that we really need to get three times consent. People who slap should learn how to do it safely, and you would never slap someone on an ear. Before the role play, the slapper would ask, are you sure you have no triggers from childhood? Have you ever been slapped before? If so, under what circumstances?

She also said:

> It's reported that Schneiderman called one of his partners his "brown slave" and demanded that she repeat that she was his property. Race play is just as, if not more, delicate a negotiation than master-slave . . . They are not entered into casually. Or when drunk.

Governor Cuomo announced the appointment of a special prosecutor to investigate Eric: Madeline Singas, the Nassau County district attorney, who had a great deal of experience with domestic violence. I started to think about what outcome I might want. I had already accomplished my personal goals, but I knew I didn't want to roll back the clock to when people weren't investigated after serious allegations had been aired in the court of public opinion.

For the moment, I put thoughts of the investigation out of my head and boarded a plane to England, where no one would care about the story. I stayed with a cousin in London for a night, and then went to visit another cousin and his family in Cambridge. On the train, I was reading *Writing a Woman's Life*, by Carolyn Heilbrun, in which she captures, among other things, the difficulties women historically faced in speaking their truths. Women conformed to the vision to which men and society confined them. Heilbrun describes the American poet May Sarton, who felt dismayed by her own memoir *Plant Dreaming Deep*, "as she came to realize that none of the anger, passionate struggle, or despair of her life was revealed in the book." Heilbrun explains: "She had not intentionally concealed her pain: she had written in the old genre of female autobiography, which tends to find beauty even in pain and to transform rage into spiritual acceptance ... [S]he had unintentionally been less than honest." *Plant Dreaming Deep* was published in 1968. By the time Sarton published her next book, *Journal of a Solitude*, times had changed. It was 1973—Women's Equality Day was introduced in and confirmed by Congress; *Roe v. Wade* legalized abortion. In *Journal*, Sarton laid bare all her pain and depression. She showed the reader her truer self.

I paused while reading Heilbrun's book to look out the window and gaze at the lush English countryside. I felt safe. After I arrived in Cambridge, I played with my twin nieces. That night my cousin and I watched *Battle of the Sexes*, the one movie we could find that neither of us had seen and both were interested in. Set in 1973, it was about the epic tennis match between Billie Jean King and Bobby Riggs—which King won.

The next morning, I walked around Cambridge University. I stopped in a fudge store. As I bought myself a piece of salted caramel, I thought about how Eric hadn't wanted me to eat sweets. I felt so far away. What awaited me when I returned home?

More news related to my story was breaking in America. A lawyer, Peter Gleason, claimed to have information about Eric's abuse of two other women many years before me, information that had been given to him by Trump's personal lawyer Michael Cohen. Because of the investigations swirling around Cohen, Gleason didn't want to get caught up in the Schneiderman mess. According to the *New York Times*, Gleason said that Mr. Cohen "told him that if Mr. Trump, who was thinking of running for New York governor at the time, were to be elected governor, he would help bring to light the women's accusations against Mr. Schneiderman. A deep animus had existed between the two men, prompted by a $40 million civil fraud lawsuit that Mr. Schneiderman filed against Mr. Trump's for-profit educational venture, Trump University, in August 2013."

I spoke with a friend on the phone, and she said I was like the deus ex machina. David Remnick called and asked if I knew anything about this Gleason story. I hadn't a clue.

He said, "It's like a shitty movie."

The next day was Mother's Day. I spoke to my grandmother. She said, "He referred to you as a brown person. You have a beautiful color. You have a beautiful face." I felt sorry that my family was dealing with the aftermath of the media storm.

My time in London coincided with a friend's wedding. She is Sri Lankan, and I was nervous because I was going to see many people who knew my family. But the event was a joyous, boisterous, big Sri Lankan wedding. Sri Lankans like to party; they like to dance and sing. I had a ball.

Meanwhile, I was receiving a stream of notes of support:

> On behalf of all Asian women who have been marginalized in relationships of any kind with White men, I thank you for speaking out against AG Schneiderman.

> As a survivor, I have some sense of how insane and surreal the experience is.

> I've too found myself in relationships being treated in a way that was demeaning and offended my feminist sensibilities, but yet continued on.

> I woke up this morning with the sad realization that it's totally safe to say that all of us, all women, everywhere, all ages, at one time or another or on several occasions or on a regular basis, have experienced assault and abuse of some kind from at least one man. . . . But you are also healing us, and inspiring us to speak out and to help educate our daughters and girls and our sons and boys (omg who need so much help!) about boundaries, and respect, and love for one another so that we can all work to eventually turn this thing around.

I was also surprised to receive notes from ex-boyfriends and even my ex-husband, whom I hadn't been in contact with for years. He sent this text:

Hey, I'm sorry for what you are going through, and my heart goes out to you. Sending much strength and love. As you can guess, journalists have started reaching out to me. . . . Other than expressing my support I'm not commenting (obviously). Wishing you greatest strength. As ever I admire your willingness to take a stand and be strong. The world is better for it.

Later, I sent an email to everyone who had written, in which I wrote: "Your notes of support have sustained me over the last week. I am sorry not to respond to each note individually . . . Thank you for having my back, offering me a place to hide out, asking me what I need. Knowing you are out there sending good vibes means the world to me."

On my last day in London, I was having brunch at the hotel where I was staying. A little after noon, I heard cheers from upstairs. Breaking news alerts on my phone announced that Prince Harry and Meghan Markle had said "I do." I had forgotten that the royal wedding was happening. I decided to watch the rest of the festivities. I thought of back when I dreamed that I might one day marry a prince. I also thought about how the British royal family owed reparations to the colonies it had plundered and destroyed. I wanted the gems of the Crown Jewels that had been stolen from Sri Lanka to be returned.

Before I returned to the States, I decided that I should continue to stay away from New York. The story was still exploding, and I had a few weeks before beginning my new job. Julia, who had been with me when the story appeared, invited me to join her in Tulum, Mexico, about which she was writing a book. I seized the opportunity and booked a frequent-flyer ticket.

I was happy to be in Mexico for many reasons: I was far away from the news in New York. I was also in a place that I felt Americans needed to support; the Trump administration had gone out of its way to villainize Mexico and its people.

The day after I returned home, I produced a shoot at the Museum of Modern Art. I was nervous to be in a room for the first time with people who could connect me in person with the Schneiderman story. But a woman came up to me, held my hand, and said, "There's a lot of love for you in this room. We owe you."

I heard from a friend at the *New York Times* that attempts were ongoing to discredit the story. Eric's ex-wife was working behind the scenes, sending emails to people at the paper. She evidently said that the *New Yorker* story was a "witch hunt" and that the magazine wasn't interested in hearing the other side. I told my friend that the *New Yorker* had taken great care investigating the story, and there were even more women with similar stories who were too scared to have their experiences included.

During lunch with a friend, he mentioned that I'd made it onto *The Daily Show*. I hadn't watched the clip, and when I finally did that night, I was terribly disappointed. After asking a few friends for their opinions, I sent the show's host, Trevor Noah, the following note:

Dear Mr. Noah:
First, I would like to express my admiration for you. Your humor and brilliance provide much levity and comfort to people like me.

It is because of this that I was saddened and disappointed by the way my image, name, and color were used in your May 8 episode in connection with the Eric Schneiderman story.

"If he wanted to role-play with a slave, why didn't he cast a black woman? Do you know how hard it is for us to get roles?"

With this statement on your show, you added insult to injury, and re-victimized me. The way in which my situation was described also felt oblivious to the fact that many brown people have in fact been enslaved and discriminated against for centuries, especially in the former colonies, and continue to be, especially in the Middle East.

This is not to equate the history of brown people with that of black people, especially in America. But I want to point out that people of color in different groups have suffered injustice. Post-independence, my people in Sri Lanka endured a long and brutal civil war based on ethnic conflict.

There have been many salacious reports since Jane Mayer and Ronan Farrow's story broke, but this is the only note that I am sending to voice a concern, and that is because I still admire you and hope that you understand.

All best,

Tanya

A few weeks later, I received an apology from a producer of the show.

For the most part, I ignored other negative chatter. Being off Facebook and Twitter made that easy.

The investigation by Nassau County DA Madeline Singas had begun. I met with Singas and her team at Robbie Kaplan's office. I remember being asked, "What evidence of abuse do you have?"

I responded, "I don't have photographs. My face would turn red when he slapped me. But he didn't hit me to bruise me."

I thought, as I had before, "Do I need to have been bruised to be believed?"

I also thought, "I have my memory, which is sharp. There are the stories of at least three other women that are clearly similar to mine. I have a number of friends whom I told along the way, first about his controlling behavior and drinking, then about the slapping, spitting, and verbal abuse."

Singas said that, as an investigator, she found it frustrating how high the bar was set for Eric's actions to be considered a crime. She also said, "He fooled a lot of people."

Later that summer, Samantha Bee spoke with Rebecca Traister about her experience with the Schneiderman story.

Rebecca Traister: I was hoping you could tell the story of what the hell happened on the night that it was reported that New York's attorney general had beaten women, and somehow it rebounded negatively to *Full Frontal*.

Samantha Bee: Well, we had done a piece about Schneiderman, I feel like it was seven or eight months ago, in which we characterized him as a superhero. And we owned that because he really was doing just an incredible job of bringing all the AGs together, and he was putting up such great resistance, and . . . it rhymes with Spider-Man. So we made all these animations of him, like leaping from tall

buildings, and it was a really funny piece. It was really fun
to do. I had never met him before. We sat there, we talked
for about two or three hours, and that was pretty much
it, and we built this piece around him. And then that just
quietly existed. And then the day that the piece dropped,
and I recall it dropping at 6:47 p.m., because I looked at
my watch, and I was like—I saw the headline. I was making dinner, I saw the headline and was like, "No." And
then I read the article really fast. It was just horrifying. We
learned that he had tweeted at the show that day, Eric
Schneiderman had, with the animations of himself. And
he was like, "Remember when I was on *Full* . . . ?" He literally clung to us like we were his feminist life raft.

Toward the end of the summer, I decided to visit my
mother in Los Angeles. After I arrived, while I was in my bedroom working on my computer, my mother asked, "That jerk
has not contacted you?"

I said, "He's unheard of." I meant that I hadn't heard from
him.

"I'm not your enemy, Tanya. Don't think your friends are
more important than me."

I didn't consider her my enemy. I just thought she couldn't
help but criticize me. However, I admired what she had done
to keep our family together despite the abuse she herself had
dealt with. I felt sorry for her.

She asked, "Are you seeing a psychiatrist?"

I replied, "Yes, for years."

"Sometimes they mess you up," she said—insinuating that
I was messed up. Then she added, "Just say three Hail Marys.

That's more than enough. Sometimes psychiatrists put thoughts in your head." She said if I prayed, I wouldn't be like this.

I wasn't interested in knowing what she meant by this. I said, "My entire life you have made me feel bad about myself." I couldn't do anything about my mother thinking there was something wrong with me. I couldn't do anything about her wishing I were different.

While I was at her home, she wanted me to sort through old boxes. As I sat in the garage, going through box after box, I felt overwhelmed. As much as I wanted to keep moving forward and moving on, I realized I had been through a lot—a long stretch of facing death, divorce, and then abuse. I have an aversion to self-pity. I come from a country where people have suffered greatly from war, imperialism, and natural disaster; I have nothing to complain about. But in that moment, I had to take a break from arranging my things, sit down, and cry.

After Los Angeles, I went to Portland, where I had begun the journey of coming forward. It was raining lightly when I arrived. As soon as the sun came out, I took a hike. I walked by the house that looked like a dream catcher. The air smelled so green. There was no pollution. I went down a set of stairs onto a trail. Sometimes I closed my eyes and saw a scene from my life with him. It felt far away and unreal.

I thought, "What would happen if I fell into a ravine?" It might be the right way to leave this life, lost in nature. As I exited the trail back onto the road, I heard the Beatles' "Here Comes the Sun" playing loudly in a car.

After I returned to New York, I was back at *Glamour* to make Women of the Year videos. One morning, I felt fragile. There was a clenching in my chest, a shuddering that rippled through my body. I biked from my apartment along the East River. As I approached Fulton Street, a Chinese woman on a bike raised her hand up high and waved at me. I didn't know her. I wondered if there was something wrong.

Loudly, she said, "Good morning!"

That was the unexpected event I needed.

After I docked my bike, I was walking toward the World Trade Center when a voice gently said, "Excuse me." I turned around. The woman asked, "Do you know where Broadway is?" We were on Church Street. She was a block away. I pointed her in the right direction. Then she said, "One-twenty Broadway."

My heart dropped. She was going to the building where Eric's office used to be.

I developed a fear of public speaking. I soon learned why: Many months before the story came out, I had agreed to do a private talk at a salon about art and activism. I should have backed out, but the event's organizers had been so nice in their outreach that I decided to stick with it. About an hour in, the door opened and a man poked his head in. He asked, "Is this the event?" He seemed creepy and disheveled. He was South Asian, maybe Sri Lankan. How had he gotten upstairs? The security guard wasn't supposed to let anyone in who wasn't on the list.

The woman who was hosting looked uncomfortable. She kept looking at me as if to ask what we should do.

I said to her, "We're done."

I stood up and went to the side of the room. The women gathered around me like lady bonobos protecting me. He left. We then talked about everything except the fact that this man had scared us.

In those months after the *New Yorker* piece, I managed to do a few more engagements. I emceed a gala at HERE Arts Center honoring Eve Ensler, the playwright and activist, for her work on behalf of women. I spoke at the Aspen Ideas Festival, at a town hall on freedom of expression. I attended a number of Me Too–related panels. I felt like I was incognito and wondered if people knew my story.

I heard Tarana Burke say, "Somebody should talk about how these women's lives are pulling together." She was referring to the victims of Harvey Weinstein and other men. "How's Mira Sorvino holding up?"

A few months later, I was asked to be on a Brooklyn Book Festival panel on "The Art of the Accused"—how we view art by those who have been exposed as predators. I told the organizer that I was worried about stalkers. I also said I was worried about being cornered with questions about my personal situation. She said they would have extra security and that the questions would be submitted on note cards.

A. O. Scott, the film critic at the *New York Times*, was on the panel. He had written about Woody Allen in the context of Me Too. I thought about how Eric loved Woody Allen movies. When he played them on the television, I would cringe; I had stopped watching Woody Allen movies after Allen started sleeping with his longtime partner Mia Farrow's adopted daughter, Soon-Yi Previn, whom he later married.

On the panel, I said that we have a perpetrator on the Supreme Court, not knowing that hours later we would learn that with the nomination of Brett Kavanaugh, we would potentially be having *another* perpetrator on the Supreme Court.

Later at the festival, I went to hear the author N. K. Jemisin speak. One of her comments resonated strongly with me: "We craft these predatory systems in which a few people benefit and most people struggle."

Back at my apartment building, I bumped into a neighbor. He said, "We haven't seen you in a while. We wanted to say sorry for what happened. And we support you."

I said, "Thank you."

"I hope it's okay that I'm saying something."

"Yes, it's human. Thank you."

I continued to stay in touch with Jane Mayer and Ronan Farrow. They wanted to do a follow-up story about Eric, especially when the results of Singas's investigation were announced. They had more women now who wanted to share their experiences with Eric. Farrow told me he was working on a big story; he'd have to do press for a few weeks, and then he could turn his attention to the follow-up.

That big story was about CBS chairman and CEO Les Moonves and all the women whose careers fell apart because of their devastating encounters with him. It broke while I was with a friend on a train heading upstate. We sat across from each other, reading the article and giving each other horror-stricken glances. I felt triggered.

When we reached the house we had rented, we were joined by two other friends. The Moonves story was all we could talk about. One friend had worked for him. We realized that all of us had been close to or victims of predators in the workplace, which showed how pervasive the problem was. We talked about how perpetrators get away with it; they always do. That's why it keeps happening—when they get big payouts, when they have their fancy houses, when their friends don't hold them accountable, they experience no consequences.

Because of the explosion of coverage around the Moonves story, I decided to do a deep dive into the coverage around my story. I watched Jane Mayer on MSNBC, criminal defense lawyer Rikki Klieman on CBS, *CBS This Morning* cohost Gayle King's disgust with Eric calling me a "brown slave." I was fascinated and also saddened. Indeed, my name and image had been everywhere. In most instances, the news outlets had dug up old photos they found on the internet. I felt bad for the people who were in the photos with me. I wondered if they had received phone calls. I wondered if I should apologize to them.

I thought, "When I meet people who say, 'I know you; you look so familiar; we've met before,' maybe this is why."

But my presence in the news cycle had passed, and my life had gone on. Moreover, I had learned a lot about how to deal with abuse, how to come forward—and how the laws covering intimate partner violence needed to change.

CHAPTER 14

THE LESSON

While I was working on this chapter, I went to see Heidi Schreck's show *What the Constitution Means to Me*. I wasn't prepared for how much the play was about the history of violence against women. Schreck explores the legacy of trauma passed down from generation to generation among the women in her family and sets it against the backdrop of the institutionalized inequality of women in America. She talks about her guilt over being the first generation in her family not to experience violence. She talks about the failure of this country to ratify the Equal Rights Amendment and how her mother cried about that failure. At one point, she says, "When will white women stop betraying women?" She is referring to both implicit and explicit ways in which white women support the patriarchy and suppress a woman's right to choose and to live the life she wants to live.

Forty-seven percent of white women voted for Trump. If they hadn't voted for him, I believe the seismic reckoning wouldn't have begun. The misogyny, as well as the racism, he unleashed revealed the wounds America has tried too long to conceal, and at last we had an opportunity to redress them. As Rebecca Traister wrote, "One year after Donald Trump had faced no repercussions for having admitted to grabbing women nonconsensually, women appeared hell-bent on ensuring that other men *would* be forced—at long last—to accept some consequence."

Joshua Green, in his book *Devil's Bargain*, describes his experience with white supremacist and former presidential advisor Steve Bannon watching the TIME'S UP action at the Golden Globes. "It's a Cromwell moment!" Bannon said. "It's even more powerful than populism. It's deeper. It's primal. It's elemental. The long black dresses and all that—this is the Puritans. It's anti-patriarchy. You watch. The time has come. Women are gonna take charge of society."

Bannon had in part orchestrated the successful manipulation of America through populist tactics that relied on sowing fear and division. Suketu Mehta, the author of *This Land Is Our Land: An Immigrant's Manifesto*, has said, "Populists tell false stories well. We have to tell true stories better."

My favorite storyteller is Betty Reid Soskin, the oldest living National Park Service ranger and a civil rights activist. She told me about her own experience in a physically and emotionally abusive relationship. We also talked about the current chaos in our country. At the age of ninety-eight, Soskin has witnessed many periods of tumult. She talked about how this period, like previous ones, is when democracy is being redefined, and we all have access to the reset buttons.

Cultural critic Elizabeth Méndez Berry told me, with regard to awareness around intimate violence, "We're taught to be ashamed, we're taught it's our fault. So many people have been silent about their experiences for so long. Now that they're talking, it's an avalanche. The fact that so many are coming out of the shadows and sharing their stories is huge. Of course, there's lots of backlash, part of which has to do with the deliberate suppression of these stories and the pervasive idea that abuse is the exception, not an epidemic that affects millions of Americans, mostly women. That minimization is reflexive: it's what happens when the patriarchy feels threatened. I do believe in the power of telling our stories, but I also think that without profound changes in how people view women, and what they believe we deserve, we won't transform this society. The truth of the matter is that while our stories matter, if someone fundamentally does not believe that women have the right to bodily autonomy, to our own pleasure, to be valued aside from our usefulness to the men or children in our lives, then no amount of sad stories will change that. We need to shift people's worldviews, and particularly those of young men and women so they can have the beautiful, healthy, pleasurable relationships they deserve."

In the wake of Me Too and TIME'S UP, we have to look at how we raise our children, how we change the way we condition sexuality in our children, and how our culture has evolved. Patriarchy and power structures have resulted in generations of disempowered women and badly behaved men. Jennifer Friedman has spoken with me about the importance of raising boys to be feminists; boys have to go through training about how to treat women and other men with respect and kindness. Girls have to go through training about how to stand up for themselves and how to avoid situations where they might be harassed, abused, and endangered. These situations begin on the playground. As a friend said, "We are taught that if a boy hits you, it means he likes you. If he teases you, he likes you. It starts right there."

Educators play a major role in how children learn about gender dynamics, and they should go through training themselves. A friend described a disturbing experience with her daughter's teacher:

> When our daughter was in seventh grade, her "progressive" female teacher (a mother of two daughters) continually told the twelve-year-old girls that how they dressed and behaved was enticing to the male teachers and classmates. She chastised them for showing their bra straps, shoulders, and wearing shorts or skirts that she deemed too short. This was devastating to many of the girls in her class.

But numerous positive examples have emerged around the country, too. In his *New York Times* article "Boy Talk: Breaking Masculine Stereotypes," Andrew Reiner discussed training programs for boys "about the ways to recognize and prevent sexual and gendered violence" and to help them navigate relationships in the Me Too era. He mentioned a weekly lunchtime boys' group at the Sheridan School, a K–8 private school in northwest Washington, DC, and a program called Becoming a Man (BAM) for high school students on Chicago's South Side. As professor and activist Brittney Cooper has written, "In every part of their lives, young men need access to conversations about what it means to be a man in ways that are not rooted in power, dominance, and violence."

Parents can educate their children more about gender and violence. A mother wrote to The Ethicist's Kwame Anthony Appiah, of the New York Times, "Should I warn my daughter about my abusive ex-husband?" She said, "His behavior toward me through the years was a combination of putting me down and building himself up. It was often so extreme that I questioned my own perceptions of it . . . He gave me a black eye when I was pregnant and intimidated me in other less overt ways." The woman was concerned that while it was important for her daughter to have a relationship with her father, "he doesn't actually care about her and is only ensuring her loyalty in case he needs it in the future."

Appiah responded, "It is sad how many people are manipulated into staying in abusive relationships, and I'm so sorry to hear about your experience. Your daughter is right: he's the only father she has and her relationship with him is different from yours. But if your account of his behavior is accurate, you're right, too—there's reason for concern that someone as damaged as he is could play a destructive role in her life. So you do have good reason to warn her. You simply need to be very clear, in your own mind, that your interest is in protecting her and not in punishing him."

But how can any of us feel protected if our government doesn't seem to care enough about the treatment of women to make long-lasting, systemic progress? As survivors' advocate Rachna Khare pointed out to me, "The White House quietly changed the definition of domestic violence to only include harms that constitute a felony or misdemeanor crime. This would ignore psychological, emotional, financial, and verbal abuse and control. I'm worried that we're going backward and that we need bipartisan leadership to merely get us back to where we used to be."

In June 2019, E. Jean Carroll came forward with credible allegations that she had been assaulted and raped by Donald J. Trump about twenty-three years before, in a dressing room at Bergdorf Goodman. If Carroll had come forward at the time of the incident, Trump might not have gone on to become president. Surveillance video might have caught the attack on tape. But who am I kidding? He was caught on audiotape bragging about grabbing women by the pussy and getting away with it, and that didn't stop him.

Jia Tolentino wrote in the *New Yorker*:

> In her essay for *New York*, Carroll acknowledges the risk that she might make Trump more popular by telling the story of how he raped her. In these cases, the accuser is not so much disbelieved as conscripted into a narrative of women attempting to victimize men by arousing public sympathy. The powerful solidify their power by pretending that they have been threatened and attacked. This dynamic is central to both fascism and abuse.

Unsurprisingly, Trump went on the attack, claiming Carroll was not his type and that they hadn't met, that she was trying to get publicity. Certainly, some people use movements to build platforms for themselves rather than using their own platforms to elevate movements. But the vast majority of those coming forward do so at great risk to themselves. They are standing on the right side of history.

In her book, *Make Trouble*, former Planned Parenthood president Cecile Richards writes, "Fighting for what you believe in can be discouraging, defeating, and sometimes downright depressing. But it can also be powerful, inspiring, fun, and funny—and it can introduce you to people who will change your life." She also writes, "The fights we're facing—for affordable health care, equal rights, bodily autonomy, and more—are never fully won. But the lasting legacy of this moment will be the generation of women it has inspired and energized."

Recently, I saw a young performance artist do a show about male fragility. She talked about how she had learned what it was like to live in a time when "the biggest gaslighting, abusive boyfriend you've ever had is president." About being an activist, she said, "We can take a break when we don't live in a misogynist dystopia."

Journalist Richard Morgan wrote in *Time Out*:

> So far, the newfound freedom of shattered silence that has rocked all corners of the culture—in Hollywood, in Washington and in establishment art circles in New York—has effectively ended the careers of Charlie Rose, Louis C.K., Kevin Spacey, Russell Simmons, Mario Batali, Matt Lauer, top officials at WNYC and NPR, longtime maestros at the Metropolitan Opera and New York City Ballet, a major writer at the prestigious *New Yorker* magazine, and three sitting members of Congress (just to name a few). What fresh hell awaits us in tomorrow's news?

The stream of perpetrators being outed has been relentless and could be endless. What's important, however, is not to fixate on individual cases but to focus on rooting out the mindset that encourages harmful behavior. It's going to take a long time, but I think we can get to a safer world, and I find hope in this statistic: An October 2018 article in the *New York Times* cited that at the time, at least two hundred prominent men had "lost their jobs after public allegations of sexual harassment . . . Forty-three percent of their replacements were women. Of those, one-third are in news media, one-quarter in government, and one-fifth in entertainment and the arts." The piece went on to mention examples such as Robin Wright replacing Kevin Spacey on the television show *House of Cards* and Jennifer Salke replacing Roy Price as the head of Amazon Studios.

I find hope in young activists such as Jaclyn Corin, Emma González, and Naomi Wadler, who are holding adults accountable for the world they are leaving their children. I find hope in women running for office. In 2019, Congress comprised a record number of women, 24.5 percent of total voting members. Perhaps one day we might get closer in terms of female representation to countries such as Sweden, where "women now represent 46 percent of the parliament and 50 percent of the government's cabinet, with gender equality often the norm at other layers of government." Until we take the reins and exemplify what it means to be true public servants, we will not get to a more equitable world.

Catharine MacKinnon, in the *Atlantic*, wrote:

> The world's first mass movement against sexual abuse, #MeToo took off from the law of sexual harassment,

quickly overtook it, and is shifting cultures everywhere, electrifyingly demonstrating butterfly politics
in action. The early openings of the butterflies' wings
were the legal, political, and conceptual innovations
of the 1970s, but it is the collective social intervention
of the #MeToo movement that is setting off the cata-
clysmic transformations of which a political butterfly
effect is capable.

I find inspiration among those who took far bigger risks
than I had to and paved the way. In an interview by Poppy
Harlow of CNN, Supreme Court justice Ruth Bader Ginsburg said she believed the Me Too movement "will have 'staying
power' and that she doesn't worry about a serious backlash."
Ginsburg noted, "It's amazing that for the first time, women
are really listened to because sexual harassment had often been
dismissed as 'well, she made it up.'"
    Ginsburg has long been a beacon for me. My first job out
of college was at Columbia Law School. Ginsburg had recently
been appointed to the Supreme Court when she came to her
alma mater to give a talk. I listened, rapt, like everyone else.
During the audience Q&A, I stood up and asked a question—I
can't even remember what, but I remember saying that I loved
her. I was in my early twenties.
    Another beacon for me has been Anita Hill. I was in col-
lege when the Clarence Thomas confirmation hearings were
taking place. In a 2018 feature in *New York* magazine about
women and power, Hill said, "Everyone likes to remind me that
I did not win. I like to say I won, because I shared my story and
people became much more aware of a problem that has been

plaguing all of us." In her 1991 testimony about her former employer, Thomas, she said, "He spoke about acts that he had seen in pornographic films involving such matters as women having sex with animals and films showing group sex or rape scenes. . . . On several occasions, Thomas told me graphically of his own sexual prowess."

In a May 9, 2019, op-ed for the *New York Times*, Hill described the devastating effect of the hearings: "If the Senate Judiciary Committee, led then by Mr. Biden, had done its job and held a hearing that showed that its members understood the seriousness of sexual harassment and other forms of sexual violence, the cultural shift we saw in 2017 after #MeToo might have begun in 1991—with the support of the government . . . Sexual violence is a national crisis that requires a national solution . . . This crisis calls for all leaders to step up and say: 'The healing from sexual violence must begin now. I will take up that challenge.'"

Biden and his colleagues suppressed reports by other women about Thomas and blocked the testimony of women such as Sukari Hardnett, who, like Hill, had worked under Thomas at the Equal Employment Opportunity Commission. Hill was forced to take the hit on her own. Decades later, Biden made what struck me as a half-baked attempt to diminish his part in Hill's unfair treatment. At the 2019 Biden Courage Awards, he said, "I wish I could have done something . . . To this day I regret I couldn't come up with a way to get her the kind of hearing she deserved." But the damage of putting a sexual predator on the Supreme Court cannot be undone by an apology.

In 2018, when the Senate confirmed Brett Kavanaugh as a Supreme Court justice despite credible allegations of sexual assault by him from multiple women, Dr. Christine Blasey Ford in particular, history repeated itself. Kavanaugh's denials verged on the lunatic. As Jane Mayer remarked in an interview by Molly Langmuir for *Elle*, "Almost everybody was a jerk in high school in some way, right? For me, what was much more important was how he deals with the truth about who he was. And the fact that he couldn't means you've got somebody on the court who, I think almost certainly, lied under oath."

Prior to the 2018 hearings, Anita Hill wrote an op-ed for the *New York Times* titled "How to Get the Kavanaugh Hearings Right":

> [I]t's impossible to miss the parallels between the Kavanaugh confirmation hearing of 2018 and the 1991 confirmation hearing for Justice Clarence Thomas. In 1991, the Senate Judiciary Committee had an opportunity to demonstrate its appreciation for both the seriousness of sexual harassment claims and the need for public confidence in the character of a nominee to the Supreme Court. It failed on both counts.

I vividly recall the day of Dr. Ford's testimony. I happened to be in Washington, DC, for meetings at Planned Parenthood. Everyone in the office seemed shaken up, and I was especially affected by the sight of young women crying. In Dr. Ford's written and verbal testimony, she said:

> I am here today not because I want to be. I am terrified. I am here because I believe it is my civic duty to tell you what happened to me while Brett Kavanaugh and I were in high school. . . . When I got to the top of the stairs, I was pushed from behind into a bedroom. I couldn't see who pushed me. Brett and Mark came into the bedroom and locked the door behind them. There was music already playing in the bedroom. It was turned up louder by either Brett or Mark once we were in the room. I was pushed onto the bed and Brett got on top of me. He began running his hands over my body and grinding his hips into me. I yelled, hoping someone downstairs might hear me, and tried to get away from him, but his weight was heavy. Brett groped me and tried to take off my clothes. . . . I believed he was going to rape me. I tried to yell for help. When I did, Brett put his hand over my mouth to stop me from screaming. This was what terrified me the most, and has had the most lasting impact on my life. It was hard for me to breathe, and I thought that Brett was accidentally going to kill me.

Similar to what happened with the Thomas hearings, multiple women did not get to tell their stories about Kavanaugh. And both Jane Mayer and Ronan Farrow said there were other women too scared to come forward. Under these circumstances, Kavanaugh's confirmation was a fait accompli.

What might happen if we reach a majority in Congress that actually believes in truth over party loyalty? Might Thomas and Kavanaugh be impeached? A 2017 *Time*/SurveyMonkey poll "found that Republicans were significantly more likely to excuse sexual misdeeds in their own party. The survey found that while a majority of Republicans and Democrats agree that a Democratic Congressman accused of sexual harassment should resign (seventy-one percent and seventy-four percent respectively), when the accused offender was in the GOP, only fifty-four percent of Republicans would demand a resignation (compared to eighty-two percent of Democrats)."

Nonetheless, there have been positive steps on both sides of the political aisle. Congress has passed rules mandating sexual harassment training in both branches. After allegations about US Appeals Court judge Alex Kozinski became public, Supreme Court Chief Justice John Roberts "called for a special working group to examine procedures for employee complaints." Outside of government, the Academy of Motion Picture Arts and Sciences has issued a new code of conduct. Dawn Hudson, its CEO, said in a statement, "There is no place in the Academy for people who abuse their status, power or influence in a manner that violates recognized standards of decency."

Dana Goodyear, in an article for the *New Yorker* titled "Can Hollywood Change Its Ways?," listed encouraging developments in the entertainment industry:

- Amy Ziering, a documentarian who has made films about sexual assault in the military and on college campuses, started working on one about Hollywood.
- In response to the proliferating accusations in Hollywood, the Los Angeles District Attorney's office established a sex-crimes task force, and the police department

assigned five pairs of detectives, including experts in reviving cold cases. At least twenty-seven investigations had been opened, including at least one involving minors.

- Rotten Apples, a new website, created a database of TV shows and movies and their affiliations with those accused of misconduct.

- The *Hollywood Reporter* created a sexual misconduct beat and assigned seven reporters, who began fielding ten to fifteen tips a day.

- Creative Artists Agency, which was named in a *New York Times* piece as a critical cog in Weinstein's "complicity machine," pledged to create a legal fund with its pre–Golden Globes party budget. Another agency, WME, paid for a sexual-harassment helpline in the offices of Women in Film.

In December 2017, Anita Hill was appointed chair of the Hollywood Commission on Eliminating Sexual Harassment and Advancing Equality. In a letter to the commission's members shortly after Kavanaugh was confirmed, she wrote, "We must demonstrate that even when the government shows indifference to bias and inequality, we in our industry promise accountability. . . . We must make it unequivocally clear that if the government is not prepared to protect women from sexual violence, we in our industry will do it ourselves." In 1991, Hill had been prevented from defending the integrity of the highest judiciary in the land. In 2017, she was given the chance to reform our culture. Perhaps we will one day see a Hollywood Walk of Shame alongside the Hollywood Walk of Fame.

The bravery of Professor Hill and then Dr. Ford has helped

others speak their truth. Soon after Dr. Ford's testimony, news anchor Connie Chung wrote about her experience with sexual abuse at the hands of her family doctor—the same doctor who had delivered her:

> He drew the curtain, asking me to remove my clothes below the waist while he sat at his desk by the bay window . . . Here I was in my 20s, and I had never had a gynecological examination. I had never even seen exam stirrups before. It was extremely odd to spread my legs and dig my heels into those cold iron stirrups . . . While I stared at the ceiling, his right index finger massaged my clitoris. With his right middle finger inserted in my vagina, he moved both fingers rhythmically. He coached me verbally in a soft voice, "Just breathe." "Ah-ah," mimicking the sound of soft breathing. "You're doing fine," he assured me.

Chung had kept the assault to herself. "All I wanted to do was bury the incident in my mind and protect my family." About revealing this story, she wrote, "Will my legacy as a television journalist for 30-plus years be relegated to a footnote? Will 'She Too' be etched on my tombstone instead? I don't want to tell the truth. I must tell the truth. As a reporter, the truth has ruled my life, my thinking. It's what I searched for on a daily working basis."

We've learned that our words help us support one another. But words are not enough. To break the inextricable link between misogyny and power, there must be graver repercussions for perpetrators. People waste time asking, "How could

So-and-So do that?" or "How can they live with themselves?" Charlie Rose, Les Moonves—sure, they've been shamed, but their money buys them impunity. Take it away. Stop the golden parachutes. There must also be reparations for victims. Make the perpetrators pay for their victims' legal and therapy bills. Make them pay for every year their victims have to deal with the trauma after the abuse. In addition, scrutinize and publicize the investment portfolios and charitable donations of perpetrators. Make them donate their money to organizations that advocate for the health and safety of women, girls, LGBTQIA+ people, and all vulnerable communities.

As of this writing, millions of dollars remain in Eric Schneiderman's campaign fund—hundreds of thousands of dollars of which he has used to pay for his legal bills. He has also turned this fund into a private philanthropic foundation; I heard that he has reached out to organizations to offer large sums of money. A source told me that the head of one organization was reluctant to accept the donation out of concern that it would be used to redeem Eric. My opinion is that the funds should have been offered back to the original donors, so they could redistribute the money to organizations of their choosing. It shouldn't be up to Eric to decide where that money goes.

Meanwhile, the bar is set too high for perpetrators to be charged with a crime. Our laws and legal process are not on the victim's side. I do believe in redemption; I believe in restorative justice. If a perpetrator has acknowledged their crime and/or done the time, then perhaps we can be open. But most perpetrators have not done either.

The case of Jeffrey Epstein—pals with Ron Burkle, Bill

Clinton, Donald Trump, Harvey Weinstein, et al.—is off-the-charts disturbing. Julie K. Brown of the *Miami Herald* wrote a series of explosive pieces digging through the rubble of collusion and corruption that allowed Epstein to get away with heinous crimes. There was ample evidence of him "assembling a large, cult-like network of underage girls—with the help of young female recruiters—to coerce into having sex acts." The girls were mostly thirteen to sixteen years old, and there were dozens, potentially hundreds of them.

Epstein spent only thirteen months in jail, for most of which he was on work release twelve hours a day, six days a week, "despite explicit sheriff's department rules stating that sex offenders don't qualify for work release." The Miami federal prosecutor who arranged the deal and prevented justice for the victims was Alexander Acosta, who went on to become Trump's secretary of labor, which gave him oversight of labor laws, including those pertaining to human trafficking.

Bradley Edwards, a former state prosecutor who represented some of Epstein's victims, said, "The damage that happened in this case is unconscionable. How in the world, do you, the U.S. attorney, engage in a negotiation with a criminal defendant, basically allowing that criminal defendant to write up the agreement?"

Because of Brown's courageous and intrepid reporting, the Epstein case was reopened in the Southern District of New York (SDNY). In July 2019, Epstein was arrested and denied bail, and Acosta was forced to resign as secretary of labor. The SDNY investigation revealed more underage victims who had been sexually abused in Epstein's Upper East Side mansion, which had once belonged to billionaire fashion mogul Les Wexner. Along with Wexner, multiple associates were linked to Epstein—Trump, Clinton, billionaire investor Leon Black, British royal Prince Andrew, Prince Mohammed bin Salman of Saudi Arabia (who ordered the 2018 murder of journalist Jamal Khashoggi), and Alan Dershowitz (Epstein's former lawyer). Some tried to defend themselves by claiming that they hadn't been in touch with Epstein for a long time. But what kind of defense was this? So what if they had no contact with him after he became a liability—what about all the years before they stopped talking to him?

In early August, documents were released in a defamation suit filed by Epstein victim Virginia Roberts Giuffre against his "madam" and fixer, Ghislaine Maxwell. More and more high-profile men, including hedge-fund billionaire Glenn Dubin and New Mexico governor Bill Richardson, were implicated by Giuffre, although unsurprisingly they denied her claims. The day after the document dump, Epstein was found dead in his jail cell, and his passing was ultimately determined by the coroner to be a suicide. Whether it was a suicide or a hit, whether he had been told to kill himself or didn't want to face the consequences of his actions, closure for his victims was temporarily denied. But closure doesn't come through confronting one's abuser. Closure comes through justice.

As I read article after article about the Epstein case, I thought, "The rage of the victims might now be unleashed with infinite force, and perhaps they will tell more. Perhaps Maxwell and other accomplices will go to trial and face the victims' testimonies." I also thought, "We need a civil war—between feminists and patriarchs." Those on the side of the feminists are not only women, and those on the side of the patriarchs are not only men.

When the devastating docuseries *Surviving R. Kelly* came out in early 2019, it at last blew the lid off the longstanding open secret that the singer had entrapped and abused women and girls for years in his own personal sex cult. Until the series, Kelly had been a pop-culture icon with hit after hit, collaborating with the likes of Lady Gaga and Celine Dion, despite decades of allegations, legal actions, and video evidence against him. A campaign to #MuteRKelly, first begun in 2017, forced radio stations to stop playing his music and his record label, RCA, to drop him. The fallout went even further, with Kelly being arrested on fresh charges and held without bond.

In an op-ed for the *New York Times*, the sisters Salamishah and Scheherazade Tillet, founders of the Chicago-based organization A Long Walk Home, which combats violence against women and girls, and consultants on the series, wrote, "Over the past week, we've had conversations with many people who had never believed black girls' allegations against [Kelly] until they saw the documentary." John Legend, who appeared in the series, posted on Twitter: "To everyone telling me how courageous I am for appearing in the doc, it didn't feel risky at all. I believe these women and don't give a f*** about protecting a serial child rapist. Easy decision."

The musician Ryan Adams had to face his own bad behavior toward women and girls he preyed upon, after an exposé by Joe Coscarelli and Melena Ryzik of the *New York Times*. A fourteen-year-old girl named Ava, an aspiring bass player, said,

"I was really alone, and he was really friendly and cool." She talked about video calls during which Adams would expose himself. Coscarelli and Ryzik wrote, "For Ava, the idea that she would be objectified or have to sleep with people to get ahead 'just totally put me off to the whole idea' of being a musician, she said. She never played another gig." Adams also solicited Courtney Jaye, a thirty-five-year-old artist, with offers to collaborate, but when they got together to make music, he moved in on her. Jaye said, "Something changed in me that year. It made me just not want to make music."

Another of Adams's accusers, musician Phoebe Bridgers, posted on Instagram: "Ryan had a network too. Friends, bands, people he worked with. None of them held him accountable . . . They validated him. He couldn't have done this without them." Coscarelli and Ryzik explained, "The music world, in which a culture of late nights and boundary-pushing behavior has been normalized, hasn't been as roiled by the #MeToo movement as other sectors of media and entertainment." As a result of their article, the FBI launched an investigation into Adams's sexting with underage girls, and the release of his new album was stopped.

Typically, however, perpetrators don't face serious financial or legal consequences, and they deny the allegations, even when these are independently investigated and thoroughly corroborated. That happened with Eric Schneiderman immediately after my story came out. In some instances, perpetrators have the gall to see themselves as victims. (Russell Simmons, for one, posted #NotMe when he was exposed by Jenny Lumet's horrific account of being assaulted by him.) They seem to think they're good guys, and that the women merely misinterpreted their actions. And many miss the limelight. As Glenn Whipp wrote in the *Los Angeles Times*:

> Louis C.K. has performed sets at the Comedy Cellar. Matt Lauer is taking meetings. Charlie Rose reportedly pitched a show in which he'd interview other men brought down by the #MeToo movement. These men and many others caught up in allegations of sexual misconduct lost their jobs, their reputations and their privilege. What most of them haven't lost is the conviction that they—not the women who decided to no longer suffer in silence—are the real victims and, as such, do not need forgiveness.

Not long after multiple allegations came out about Tavis Smiley and his PBS show was canceled, he went on the road with an "inspirational" series called *The Upside with Tavis Smiley* and a five-city "town hall" tour to talk about relationships in the workplace. Accused journalist John Hockenberry wrote a "poor me" piece for *Harper's*, and radio host Jian Ghomeshi wrote one for the *New York Review of Books*. These publications made disastrous decisions to give platforms to the accused when they could have given platforms to their victims.

In many instances, perpetrators have attempted to wash their dirty laundry with philanthropy, as in the case of Ron Burkle hosting benefits for rape crisis centers and Harvey Weinstein supporting Planned Parenthood. Jeffrey Epstein called himself a "celebrated philanthropist" and "renowned educational investor." In 2012, he undertook "a public relations campaign to counter bad press about his sexual exploits" and donated "millions to scientific research."

Perpetrators and their enablers harbor each other even after they've been exposed. During the 2019 Sundance Film Festival, David Glasser, the former president and chief operating officer for the Weinstein Company, announced that he was starting a new production company with the backing of . . . Ron Burkle. Meanwhile, filmmaker John Lasseter, after being dumped by Pixar for his inappropriate behavior toward women and his creation of a fratlike atmosphere, went on to be hired by Skydance Media, a production company under Paramount Animation. Female employees were told they could choose to decline to work with him. The actress Emma Thompson took a stand and pulled out of a Skydance project with a pointed letter:

> It feels very odd to me that you and your company would consider hiring someone with Mr. Lasseter's pattern of misconduct given the present climate in which people with the kind of power that you have can reasonably be expected to step up to the plate.
>
> I realise that the situation—involving as it does many human beings—is complicated. However, these are the questions I would like to ask:
>
> • If a man has been touching women inappropriately for decades, why would a woman want to work for him if the only reason he's not touching them inappropriately now is that it says in his contract that he must behave "professionally"?
>
> • If a man has made women at his companies feel

undervalued and disrespected for decades, why should the women at his new company think that any respect he shows them is anything other than an act that he's required to perform by his coach, his therapist and his employment agreement? The message seems to be, "I am learning to feel respect for women so please be patient while I work on it. It's not easy."

In Naomi Alderman's book *The Power*, a girl takes her first piano lesson, and the piano teacher sticks his hands down her underpants and tells her to be quiet and keep playing. She tells her dad, who then beats the shit out of the teacher. Every time the teacher sees the girl he is struck with fear. It's tempting to think of this approach as a solution, but violence begets violence.

Perpetrators have to suffer tangible consequences, yet the law often lets them get away with it. Inadequate legal frameworks, including the US Constitution, need to be updated. As critic Ginia Bellafante pointed out about New York State's laws:

> Felony assault in New York State requires the demonstration of significant injury—a broken limb, a gunshot wound, serious impact to an organ. If none of these can be proved, a prosecutor might then move on to consider misdemeanor assault, and here, too, she might run into trouble. . . . A prosecutor would have to prove that there was intent to cause physical injury. Disturbingly, the requirement of "intent"

allows nearly anyone accused of beating someone up during consensual sex to claim he was doing so for the purpose of arousal.

Moreover, the United States has not ratified the Equal Rights Amendment. Justice Ginsburg has said, "Equal stature of men and women is as fundamental as the basic human rights . . . every Constitution in the world written since the year 1950 has the equivalent statement that men and women are people of equal citizenship stature." Catharine MacKinnon has written that "the only legal change in U.S. law that matches the [#MeToo] movement's scale would be the passage of an Equal Rights Amendment. That would, at minimum, expand the congressional power to legislate against sexual abuse. It could renovate interpretations of equality in a more substantive and intersectional direction, reconfiguring the concept by guaranteeing sex equality for all under the Constitution for once."

With regard to workplace protections, as Alieza Durana pointed out in an article for the *Atlantic*, as much as 18 percent of the US labor force is not covered by Title VII of the 1964 Civil Rights Act, which recognizes two categories of harassment. One category is "when a boss, supervisor, or anyone in a position of authority with hiring or firing abilities pressures a subordinate for sexual favors in exchange for a promotion or raise, or to avoid dismissal." The second category is "a hostile work environment created by severe or pervasive harassment, which could include repeated lewd comments and off-color jokes, unwanted sexual advances, or even sexual assault." But Title VII does not apply to small businesses (i.e., businesses of

fewer than fifteen employees), agricultural and domestic workers, or independent contractors.

A World Health Organization paper on violence by intimate partners highlighted the difficulty of quantifying and
qualifying the issue because of inconsistencies in reporting
practices and because of the unwillingness of some victims to
share their experiences. To improve disclosure, the paper suggested the following:

- Giving the interviewee several opportunities during an
  interview in which to disclose violence
- Using behaviorally specific questions, rather than subjective questions such as "Have you ever been abused?" [An
  example of a behaviorally specific question was "Have
  you ever been forced to have sexual intercourse against
  your will?"]
- Carefully selecting interviewers and training them to
  develop a good rapport with the interviewees
- Providing support for interviewees, to help avoid retaliation by an abusive partner or family member

The paper also addressed the importance and success of
treatment programs for perpetrators. According to research
from the United States, the majority of men in treatment
programs "remain physically non-violent for up to two years,
with lower rates for longer follow-up periods." But there was
a high dropout rate of between one-third and one-half of men
who enrolled in the programs, and many who were referred
never enrolled. The paper cited the need for accountability
through criminal justice measures. Pittsburgh, Pennsylvania,

for example, "began issuing arrest warrants for men who failed to appear at the program's initial interview session." As a result, its nonattendance rate "dropped from thirty-six percent to six percent between 1994 and 1997."

In addition to strengthening laws and centering victims in policymaking, we must improve our reporting and monitoring mechanisms. Power systems lend themselves to corruption and abuse. CBS protected Les Moonves, Fox protected Roger Ailes, NBC protected Matt Lauer, and the list goes on and on. Monitoring has to happen outside the system. And the reporting process has to be less cumbersome and intimidating; "human resources" too often means "corporate resources."

Jennifer Friedman has spoken with me about how the legal system often revictimizes victims. Even when women are believed, there is so much in our culture that rakes women over the coals. The victim is picked apart and questioned. It's one of the reasons that women feel silenced. Friedman told me about a woman in law school who was date raped. The victim did not want to come forward because she did not want to be easily identified; she didn't want future employers to google her and know she was a victim. In another story, a woman who had just graduated from college was drugged and anally raped; she woke up the next morning bleeding and in pain. The perpetrator claimed their sex was consensual. Friedman had been advocating with a district attorney's office who declined to prosecute. Friedman said it was likely the perpetrator had drugged and raped other women as well.

While I was working on this chapter, a young female friend was brutally raped and beaten. The perpetrator was a stranger.

He tried to kill her, but she got away. When I saw her afterward, she looked like a zombie. He had broken some of her teeth and given her two black eyes and multiple wounds on her face. After almost two weeks, the perpetrator was caught. I hope that he will be locked up for life. Otherwise, he will probably rape and try to kill someone else. I do think there should be a special place in hell for sexually violent people.

I am reminded of the despicable case of Brock Turner, who in 2015, while a student at Stanford University, assaulted an unconscious woman by a dumpster. He ended up serving only three months of the already paltry six-month sentence he received. His father had the indecency to say that Turner shouldn't suffer for "twenty minutes of action," meaning the time during which his son assaulted the woman. What his father and many don't understand is that whether the abuse lasts twenty minutes, a day, a month, a year, or decades, the scars of being harassed, assaulted, raped, and brutalized leave an indelible impact. Moments of abuse mark time before and after.

As media critic Soraya Chemaly has written, "Men learn to regard rape as a moment in time; a discreet [sic] episode with a beginning, middle, and end. But for women, rape is thousands of moments that we fold into ourselves over a lifetime." What Oprah Winfrey said, when speaking about Michael Jackson's victims, applies universally: "The emphasis should not be on the sex act itself, but what happens afterwards. . . . It is the holding of the secret, it is the shame, it is the confusion, it is the guilt, the depression, and then the nervous breakdown that happens to so many people."

Brock Turner's survivor read a letter at his trial:

I used to pride myself on my independence, now I am afraid to go on walks in the evening, to attend social events with drinking among friends where I should be comfortable being. I have become a little barnacle always needing to be at someone's side, to have my boyfriend standing next to me, sleeping beside me, protecting me. It is embarrassing how feeble I feel, how timidly I move through life, always guarded, ready to defend myself, ready to be angry.

In closing, she said:

[T]o girls everywhere, I am with you. . . . As the author Anne Lamott once wrote, "Lighthouses don't go running all over an island looking for boats to save; they just stand there shining." Although I can't save every boat, I hope that by speaking today, you absorbed a small amount of light, a small knowing that you can't be silenced, a small satisfaction that justice was served, a small assurance that we are getting somewhere, and a big, big knowing that you are important, unquestionably, you are untouchable, you are beautiful, you are to be valued, respected, undeniably, every minute of every day, you are powerful and nobody can take that away from you.

At the time, she was anonymous, but years later, in 2019, Chanel Miller told her story through a memoir titled *Know My Name*. We can turn rage into light by advocating for change, on campuses that have become breeding grounds for perpetrators and in our communities, at the local and national levels.

My friend Catherine, in whose home I sought refuge as my story came out, sent me an email that gave me hope:

> It appears that if there is any country in the world that is swiftly headed in a progressive direction, it's New Zealand. They just passed legislation granting victims of domestic violence 10 days paid leave to allow them to leave their partners, find new homes and protect themselves and their children. *This makes them the only country in the world to do this!* Let's make it spread!

Imagine how we can make it spread. We can start by advocating for a similar law with our congresspeople. We can ask them where they stand with regard to protections for victims. We can support candidates who have the courage to build the safer world we envision for ourselves.

In the appendix of this book, with the collaboration of Jennifer Friedman, I provide suggestions for how to spot intimate partner violence, as well as resources for victims to get help. With the paradigm shift brought about by Me Too, we have been letting go of the old ways of power that have oppressed and silenced women. We are welcoming new ways. Still, it will take many seismic events in the public consciousness for progress to be made.

CHAPTER 15

MOVING FORWARD

During a phone call with my grandma, she asked how I was doing.

"I'm all right."

She said, "Give him a kick in the ass. You do it. He deserves it. I'm glad you got rid of him. Grandma is always there for you."

My grandma always tells it like it is. But in this instance, I didn't have to do anything except get on with my life and recover. The investigation of Eric was ongoing. I had supported it by speaking with the team led by Nassau County DA Madeline Singas. I was patient with the process. Eventually there would be an outcome.

I went to my high school reunion, where I found myself often observing rather than engaging. I wanted to hang back. It had not been long since my story became public; many people approached me to thank me for coming forward. One friend said she didn't expect to see me there. But I was happy to be around people who had known me for a long time.

On the ride home, I commented to my closest friend from school, Gabriela, that Massachusetts was an emotional state for me. It was where I had gone to high school, college, and graduate school. I had lived there when I was married. She reminded me that it was also where I had gone through my surgeries, at Mass General.

The day after the *New Yorker* story came out, a *New York Times* editor reached out asking if I would write an op-ed. I wrote her back: "My plan for when the article broke was to let the story speak for itself and not enter the media frenzy. So, I've been hiding." But she and I continued to stay in touch over the next few months. After Dr. Ford's testimony at the Kavanaugh hearings, I felt I was ready for an op-ed to come out. I was hopeful that I could provide a window into the process of coming forward and the trauma that never completely goes away. I called the editor and sent her a draft. Because of the especially intense news cycle, she wanted to pause to wait for a good moment to publish it.

On October 5, the *Times* editor gave me a heads-up that the piece would come out that weekend. To be safe, I moved out of my apartment again and into Catherine's home. I sent a note to my mother, brother, and sister-in-law to alert them, adding, "Maybe don't read it. But if you do, I hope it doesn't cause concern. I am absolutely doing great and feel I did the right thing." To my mother, I added, "Please don't be mad."

The piece ran on the evening of October 6, a few hours after Brett Kavanaugh was confirmed to the Supreme Court. Below is an excerpt:

> Ultimately, I take responsibility for staying, but doing
> so took a deep toll. . . . I didn't understand until

after the relationship ended how physiological the impact is—the shaking and shuddering that happens suddenly, when I feel trapped, when I feel mocked. Symptoms of post-traumatic stress are a real and common reaction to abuse. Sometimes when I look in the mirror, I hear his voice in my head belittling me. Still, while I regret getting into the relationship, I don't regret coming forward. . . . [W]e've learned this past year that our words can chip away at violence, and can challenge the way society conditions us to accept it. Recently, I have been reading Naomi Alderman's novel *The Power*, about a future society in which women discover hidden physical abilities, which includes this passage: "A dozen women turned into a hundred. A hundred turned into a thousand. The police retreated. The women shouted; some made placards. They understood their strength, all at once."

We've learned that we are not alone. We understand our strength, all at once.

I received many notes, including this one, which especially touched me, from Rachna Khare, who is cited elsewhere in this book:

Your story shook me to my core. I wanted to say thank you. Thank you for so poignantly describing the elation of love, the cycle of manipulation, and the pain of violence. It's difficult, especially in the South Asian culture, to talk about sex—even in a positive context. You pulled back the curtain not only on sexual violence, but on the nuances that we, as women of color, specifically experience.

In my work, I often find it hard to tell stories of South Asian survivors. Like all women, our identities are complex and, therefore, our experiences are multilayered. We could peel back for eternities and there would still be layers left. Your account was gripping—it was painful and also hopeful, it was compassionate but not sanitized. It was educational and also poetic, it was your truth and yet so incredibly relatable to us all. In less than 2,000 words, you captured the intersectionality, complexity, and truth of sexual violence.

We sent your piece to our clients who we are able to contact safely. A copy sits in our lobby and in our counseling offices. I want to thank you for sharing your truth and for making us feel less alone because, as you said, we can now "understand our strength all at once."

In the op-ed, I wrote about being nervous to engage in an intimate relationship again. That fear was quite acute. What if a man hit me? What if I stopped him and he told me he needed to do it to get aroused? Fortunately, I was introduced to a man who treated me so well that I felt like crying. We had first met in early 2018, but I was keeping a big secret then and nowhere near ready for a relationship. Months later, after the *New Yorker* story, he wrote, out of the blue, to check on me. I was surprised. And he continued to reach out, until eventually we met in person.

We spent a few nights together. He didn't criticize my scars, my breasts. He did not make me feel less than. He made me feel good about myself. As we drove through a canyon to a restaurant one night, an enormous owl standing on the road looked at us and flew away. Superstition dictates that an owl crossing one's path can be a warning. It could mean someone is going to die. But the owl also represents Athena, the goddess of wisdom and strategy. An owl sat beside Athena so she could see the truth. An owl guarded the Acropolis. I love owls, the way they turn their heads all around. At my place in Portland, an owl has occasionally perched on my deck and looked at me with big eyes.

Portland was where I had written my first-person narrative and made the decision to come forward. A year later, I went back there to work on this book. I had printed out hundreds of pages of notes and research. After about a week there, I felt I was ready to review the material. I was in a good place. But the notes I had recorded at the time the abuse was occurring now cut like a knife. I felt pain acutely in my gut. It was a sinking feeling. It was a caving-in feeling. It felt like my heart was burning down. It felt like hopelessness.

It wasn't just my story. It was all the stories that people had shared with me and that I had researched. I thought, "The problem will never be solved. As long as there are the constructs of money and real estate, there will be power dynamics that give rise to abuse. It doesn't matter how many laws or law enforcement officers are put in place to monitor and protect. The laws will be broken; predators will get away with it; enablers will protect them; victims will suffer."

I told no one about my depression for a few weeks. I felt

like I was spiraling. I started making plans for how to leave this world. When I had my surgeries in 2012, the hospital staff suggested I write a will, authorize a proxy to make medical decisions on my behalf, and leave a list of instructions. I put documents in an envelope that I left in my desk drawer with the words "In case of untimely death" on it. Now would I deal with the logistics of dying?

I thought of the ways: a knife, a sheet, a belt—not pills (where would I get them?), not a plunge into the hills near my house (I might be eaten by animals). Thoughts of people I knew who had attempted or succeeded in killing themselves swirled through my mind. But when the thoughts paused, I realized that either I'm here or I'm not, and I knew I had to reach out. I emailed a handful of friends that I was feeling very low and that the last two years had finally caught up with me. They rallied around me. Through their calls and notes, they helped me look out and up.

I kept writing.

During that low point, I said to my friend Farai, "The bad guys win."

She said, "But the storytellers also win."

I wrote my way out of the darkness.

CODA
(SIX MONTHS LATER)

November 7, 2018, the night after the midterm elections, Melissa Silverstein took me to the taping of *Full Frontal with Samantha Bee*. At the security check, the guard said he had to hold on to my pepper spray and that I could pick it up after the show. I had been carrying that pepper spray since April. I didn't feel fear anymore, but I had continued to keep it in my purse.

Silverstein is the founder of the advocacy group Women and Hollywood and of the Athena Film Festival at Barnard College. She gives women filmmakers a platform and calls out the ways in which the Hollywood system perpetuates inequality.

When the taping was done, the producer and correspondent of *Full Frontal* came over to say hi to Silverstein. I felt reticent as she approached. We had met when I was making the *Glamour* Women of the Year video about Bee. Would she recognize me? Would she connect me with Eric Schneiderman? But I decided to hold my head up high and thanked her.

That same night, I received a note from Robbie Kaplan, indicating that Madeline Singas was expected to make an announcement the next day about the Schneiderman investigation. In Singas's statement, she wrote, "I believe the women who shared their experiences with our investigation team; however[,] legal impediments, including statutes of limitations, preclude criminal prosecution." She also said that she had proposed a new state law to "protect victims of sexually motivated violence by making it illegal to hit, shove, slap or kick someone without their consent for 'the purpose of sexual arousal or gratification.'"

Eric also issued a statement: "I recognize that District Attorney Singas' decision not to prosecute does not mean I have done nothing wrong. I accept full responsibility for my conduct in my relationships with my accusers, and for the impact it had on them." He also said that he had been seeking help in a rehab facility and was "committed to a lifelong path of recovery and making amends to those I have harmed."

I felt this was a positive outcome: a strong statement from the DA, proposed changes in legislation, and Eric's acknowledgment of wrongdoing. These became part of an extraordinary week, alongside the midterm election results that included Letitia James becoming New York State attorney general, the first female and first African American in that position.

At the time of Singas's announcement, I was working again on the *Glamour* Awards. That same day, during the staging session, when my tribute videos were reviewed, the group spontaneously clapped for me. They were applauding the videos, but it felt like an affirmation of what I had done in coming forward.

A woman sitting next to me said suddenly, "I noticed your scar."

She pulled down her sweater to show me the center of her chest. She had a scar, too. We high-fived. She had had a bovine valve implanted. She asked me what mine was for. I told her cancer. I now felt proud of my scars. At the ceremony, I met Judge Rosemarie Aquilina, who in her courtroom had thrown away a defense letter from Larry Nassar, the sports doctor who had sexually abused so many gymnasts.

The following week, I went to Boston for my annual CT scan. In the waiting room, as happened only in that moment every year, it hit me that I felt odd being there; the others waiting were mostly much older. I could feel them looking at me. All of us might have been wondering what the others had. Every year for at least ten years, from 2012, I'm told I should have this experience. It marks time.

As I arrived at the train station to return to New York, my phone rang. It was the doctor's office. The nurse asked if I was still in Boston; the radiologist wanted me to come back for more tests. My heart dropped. Everything had gone so smoothly. Now I had about seventy-five minutes to get to the hospital and back. I doubted I could make it. If I didn't, I would be stuck in Boston for Thanksgiving, because all subsequent trains were sold out. But I did make it. The last time I had gotten a call at a train station about returning for a medical test was in 2012, when I would eventually be diagnosed with a GIST and a thymoma. But this time, when the doctor called later with the results, there was no recurrence. This time, I didn't have to stop in my tracks. I could keep moving until the next round of tests, in a year. I could work on this book.

Getting back to work, I thought about all the advice I

wished I'd been given and that I wanted to give others who are being victimized. I made a list:

- Document what is happening. Include dates and correlate them with supporting material like email exchanges and photos.
- Tell someone—ideally more than one person—whom you trust not to tell anyone else.
- Figure out whom you can speak with who will know what to do. (In my case, one friend put me in touch with Jennifer Friedman and another connected me with Robbie Kaplan.)
- Know that you are not alone and you are not crazy.
- It's okay to feel traumatized, but please don't feel ashamed.
- If your partner is not willing to acknowledge the problem *and* get professional help, get away. Your partner is probably not going to change.
- Don't worry about your abuser. Focus on yourself.
- You are the most important part of this equation.

Lastly, I would tell all women what Elizabeth Méndez Berry told me: "Put pleasure first: Learn about your own body and how to please yourself on your terms, not somebody else's. Develop a coven of feminist friends who will ride for you and challenge you, lovingly tell you the hard truths when you don't want to hear them."

While I was working on this book, my editor, Libby Burton, told me that her office was being moved to 120 Broadway, where Eric's office had been. The universe was not only trying to liberate me from a long stretch of personal and health set-backs; it was encouraging me to conquer my fear of places and situations.

After the CT scans, when I got home to New York, the place where I had been feeling trapped, where I had been in a cage for so long, I felt a leavening. On May 7 of that same year, my story of intimate violence had been revealed to the world. Six months later, I felt free.

APPENDIX

Jennifer Friedman, the director of the legal project at two family justice centers in New York City for Sanctuary for Families, was my sounding board and guide throughout the strenuous process of extracting myself from an abusive relationship and strategizing for my safety. We met in person in the spring of 2019 to brainstorm for this appendix. The day was May 7, exactly one year since the *New Yorker* story. (Friedman and I had picked the date by coincidence.) We began by exchanging a hug.

I asked Friedman to collaborate with me to provide an accessible, easy-to-digest resource for how to spot, stop, and prevent intimate partner violence. Below is her statement:

Every survivor's story is unique, and all survivors' experiences are intensely personal, often causing deep scars, physical and emotional, which can take a lifetime to heal. Despite this, there are commonalities among the stories I have heard from survivors I have encountered from all over the world. Domestic violence is one form of gender-based violence, which also includes sexual harassment, sexual assault, female genital mutilation, honor crimes, human trafficking, forced and child marriage, and others. Domestic violence involves a pattern of gender-based intimate partner, dating, or family violence with a central dynamic of power and control. In this dynamic, the abuser establishes and maintains power and asserts control over the victim/survivor. The manifestation of this dynamic can take many forms, including physical, sexual, emotional, economic, psychological, digital, and legal (discussed in this appendix).

Domestic violence is prevalent across demographic lines, including race, class, sexual orientation, and gender, although the vast majority of victims are women and girls. Not every abuser engages in physical violence. Many may use threats, such as threatening to take the children or to hurt family members, and the weight of those threats may be effective enough so that violence is not necessary. The abuser will be extremely skilled in homing in on the victim's weaknesses and pressure points in order to exploit and manipulate her, in asserting dominance, and in enforcing compliance. This may be psychological abuse and can include exploiting a victim's history of sexual abuse to his advantage. Once women have children, this vulnerability makes them easy prey. The abusers often will use the children as pawns and leverage, even well after the relationship has ended, when there can be extensive litigation over custody, visitation, and child support. Or, the abuser may construct a weakness in the victim over time, as in the case of cyber sexual abuse, where the abuser may take photographs of the victim and threaten to post them online or disseminate them to her family, community, or employer.

Many victims experience extreme trauma and may exhibit symptoms of post-traumatic stress disorder (PTSD). This is a normal psychological and physiological reaction to being threatened with death or severe harm, and is now understood to be a significant aspect of the experience of intimate partner violence. For example, the experience of being strangled, in which your air supply is cut off and you are unable to breathe, can invoke extreme trauma and PTSD.

Some victims experience a dynamic known as the "cycle of violence." There was a time when this cycle was thought to be the primary manifestation of domestic violence. While I do not see this as the only dynamic, it is a common pattern, in which there is an escalation of tension so that the victim feels she is "walking on eggshells" and that anything she does will set off the abuser. Finally, there is a violent incident that breaks the tension, and afterward there is a "honeymoon" period, in which the abuser begs for forgiveness and a break from the abuse follows. Over time, physical violence may not be as necessary because the threat is always there. The abuser has accomplished compliance.

Some domestic violence is a prelude to, or part of, sex trafficking, pimping, and commercial sexual exploitation. Many sex traffickers or pimps seek out vulnerable young people, often those who are homeless or living in group homes, and lure them into romantic relationships in which they are first courted and then subjected to intimate partner violence, "groomed," and pimped.

Many survivors have their first experiences of intimate partner violence as teens or young adults. Signs of abuse in young people may be similar to those in adults but often include abuse on social media, use of photos or videos to manipulate them, excessive texting, and demanding access to passwords. College dating violence is also extremely prevalent, with nearly half of dating college women reporting experiencing abusive dating behaviors, as is sexual assault both occurring within the context of intimate relationships and being exacerbated by partying and fraternity cultures.

There may be inherent or structural power imbalances in the relationship between victim and abuser that are easy to exploit, such as financial power, immigration status, health issues such as HIV status, and use of male, racial, or ethnic privilege. Whichever modality the abuser selects, the abuse is strategic, intended to exert control, and the victim may ultimately feel trapped in the relationship, finding it difficult, even impossible, to escape. The isolation has made her feel she has no friends or family to turn to. The sexual abuse has made her feel vulnerable and possibly ashamed. The emotional and psychological abuse has chipped away at her self-confidence, making her feel dependent or less capable than she really is. The economic abuse has possibly left her with no resources to survive on her own and take care of her children. The threats—to kill her, to take her children, to hurt her animals or family, to expose vulnerabilities— are very effective at instilling a fear of leaving. For immigrant victims, these dynamics are exacerbated by fear of deportation, language barriers, and lack of knowledge of victims' rights within the American legal system.

Given this web of control, it is amazing that so many victims do leave and escape. Fortunately, thanks to the brave and groundbreaking work of so many leaders and feminist pioneers over the past fifty years, there are trusted resources to turn to. There are counselors and shelters, sexual assault hotlines, legal services, and some economic-support resources, although certainly not enough. Included in this appendix are links to resources for victims in every state. I encourage anyone who reads this book and recognizes that they are in an abusive relationship to reach out to experts in the field and their community who can help develop a safety plan for their individual situation. My mantra is that because every situation is unique, it is imperative that safety planning is done individually for each victim. There isn't a cookie-cutter plan that is right for everyone. It is critical that victims and advocates be aware of danger and known lethality factors (listed in this appendix), and the reality that threats to kill can be acted upon. The most dangerous time is when the victim leaves or attempts to leave, because the abuser has lost control. This is when threats to kill become most serious, and safety planning is critical.

For Tanya, there was a powerful abuser with unusual resources at his disposal. I was especially concerned about her safety. We talked at length about her knowledge of his behavior and what she believed his reactions would be to various scenarios as we planned her extraction. We asked many questions: Should she go to the police, which would trigger a criminal investigation and likely a prosecution? Should she file for a civil order of protection in family court? How could she best extricate herself? Where should she go immediately after she left, which can be the most dangerous time? Would he retaliate? If so, what form would that take? Would he physically come after her? Attack her in the street? Show up at her place of employment? Defame her to friends, family, or employers? Does he have "dirt" on her that he could try to exploit? Would he try to sabotage her employment? For victims who are financially dependent, or who have children, there are so many additional questions: Will he cut off support? Will he show up at the children's school? Try to take them away? Abduct them? File for custody? File false abuse charges against her with child protective services? Take them to another country with different laws that favor men?

The answers to these questions and many, many more will dictate the course of action that is best for each survivor. An order of protection (the name may differ by state—restraining order, protective order, etc.) can be a powerful tool, as can be filing for custody, divorce, or child support. But it is not the right move for everyone. Are you in a shelter, effectively hidden for the moment? Then perhaps filing may not be in your best interest, as the abuser would need to be served with papers and will now have the chance to locate you and retaliate. What is your economic plan for survival? Do you need child support, or should you consider filing for public assistance? Do you want or need an order of custody? Be aware that initiating a family court case could turn into a protracted battle, and the abuser will likely be granted visitation with the children. Do you know if he is planning to file for custody anyway? Then perhaps you should file first, giving yourself the opportunity to frame the narrative. Of course, it is difficult to make these decisions without legal counsel. While the costs of an attorney may be out of reach for many victims, there are organizations that provide free legal advice, which can be accessed through the resources listed here.

Your abuser may have convinced you that you have vulnerabilities he would expose in court. Talk these through with a lawyer, if possible. It may be that there are real legal challenges, or it may be that he has manipulated you into believing that he has advantages that are not in fact legally compelling. You may also have rights you were unaware of. If you are an immigrant survivor, there are pathways to legal residency separate from the abuser, such as asylum, a Violence Against Women Act Self-Petition (aka battered spouse waiver), a U visa, a T visa, or Special Immigrant Juvenile Status (SIJS).

In any case, my strongest advice is to reach out, if possible, to one of the resources provided here and, when you feel ready, safely speak with someone who can help provide you with options you may not have known existed. You are the expert in your own situation. Your intuition is there for a reason, and you should use it to help guide you through this entire process. If you are receiving advice you doubt, perhaps you should get a second opinion. You know the pressure points and the danger you are in, and you should not allow anyone to convince you to do anything that you are not ready for. Ultimately, no one except you walks in your shoes.

All survivors have to decide for themselves whether and when they are ready to share their stories and possibly seek help. No matter how humiliating you may think your situation is, coming forward and speaking your truth, if only to a counselor or lawyer, is extraordinarily brave and can bring about a breakthrough. The abuser has sought to silence your voice and diminish your self-worth, preventing you from feeling your own power. But you *do* have power, and seeking help (including speaking with an expert) may bring you more power. Taking back your power is an important step toward healing and reclaiming your life. While the larger society may not honor women's voices because of an entrenched power structure dominated primarily by men, times are changing.

—Jennifer Friedman, Director, Bronx and Manhattan
Legal Project and Policy, Sanctuary for Families

I. Signs of Intimate Partner Violence

The following is adapted from "Interviewing and Assisting Domestic Violence Survivors," by B. J. Cling and Dorchen A. Leidholdt, in *Lawyer's Manual on Domestic Violence: Representing the Victim*, Mary Rothwell Davis, Dorchen A. Leidholdt, and Charlotte A. Watson, eds., 6th ed. (Supreme Court of the State of New York, 2015), http://ww2.nycourts.gov/sites/default/files/document/files/2018 -07/DV-Lawyers-Manual-Book.pdf.

JEALOUSY AND POSSESSIVENESS

Jealousy and possessiveness are two of the most common characteristics of abusers. These may initially be interpreted by the victim as signs of her partner's passion and devotion, though it soon becomes apparent that they underlie his acts of domination and control. The jealousy can take many different forms. An abuser may use GPS to monitor a victim, accuse her of having affairs with every man in her life, call the victim frequently during the day, send constant text messages, drop by her place of work unexpectedly, prevent her from performing her job effectively, check her car's mileage, or ask friends or neighbors to watch her.

CONTROLLING BEHAVIOR

This is a hallmark of abuse, which may be related to jealousy and can permeate every facet of existence. An abuser will initially attribute his controlling behavior to concern for her well-being. The situation will progressively worsen. The abuser may ultimately monitor her every move, assume control of all finances, or prevent the victim from coming and going freely.

QUICK INVOLVEMENT

A victim often knows or dates the abuser for a brief, intense period of time before getting engaged or moving in together. Almost immediately in their relationship, the abuser will pressure the victim to commit to him and will make her feel guilty for wanting to slow the pace. The abuser expects the partner to meet all his needs, build her world around him, and submerge her identity in his.

MANIPULATIVE BEHAVIOR

Abusers are often skilled manipulators who begin by appearing to be devoted, dependable partners. Once victims are entrapped in the relationship and try to get out, abusers may manipulate the very agencies the victims can turn to for help, such as criminal justice, child welfare, and judicial authorities. Often the abuser will succeed in having his victim investigated for child abuse or neglect, arrested for fabricated crimes, or tarred as an alienating parent. Abusers will also manipulate their own children, persuading them that their mother is to blame for the family's no longer living together or for their moving from their old neighborhood or school.

ISOLATION

Abusers isolate their victims by severing the victims' ties to outside support and resources. The abuser will create conflict with the victim's friends and family, forcing the victim to choose between them and him. The abuser may block the victim's access to use of a vehicle, work, or telephone and internet service in the home. He wants her in the home, where she is totally under his control, so any social contact becomes a threat.

BLAME AND INCESSANT CRITICISM

The abuser is never at fault and never accepts responsibility for his actions, blaming others for his own shortcomings. He will blame the victim for almost anything, including his poor work performance, his bad relationships with other people, and, above all, his violence toward her.

ABUSIVE AND VIOLENT SEX

Sexual abuse is a pervasive form of domestic violence. This includes forcing unwanted sex, restraining partners against their will during sex, acting out fantasies in which the partner is helpless, initiating sex when the partner is asleep, or demanding sex when the partner is ill or tired.

VERBAL ABUSE

Abusers usually subject their victims to an unending barrage of insults. The epithets "bitch" and "whore" are staples among abusers, as are threats and obscenities. The language the abuser uses can be cruel and hurtful, including cursing, degrading, or insulting the victim, or putting down the victim's accomplishments.

RIGID GENDER ROLES

Abusers often demand that their partners conform to traditional sex or gender roles. She is supposed to be passive, obedient, solicitous, attractive, a great cook who always has dinner on the table just when he is ready for it, and sexually available to him whenever he is in the mood. Many abusers move to control the family's finances and discourage or undermine their victims' educational and career aspirations; they maintain that marriage gives them full authority over the victim and the family.

DUAL PERSONALITY: "DR. JEKYLL AND MR. HYDE"

Abusers often exhibit different personalities at different times, leaving the victims to tiptoe around them and guess which person they will get at any given moment. At times, the abuser can be loving, and at other times cruel. Explosive behavior and moodiness can shift quickly into congeniality.

PAST BATTERING

A victim will often discover that the abuser's past relationships followed a pattern of abuse similar to hers. (Individual circumstances do not constitute an abusive personality.)

THREATS OF VIOLENCE

These consist of any threat of physical force meant to control the partner.

BREAKING OR STRIKING OBJECTS

This behavior is used as punishment (e.g., breaking sentimental possessions) or to terrorize the victim into submission.

CRUELTY TO ANIMALS

An abuser will injure or even kill beloved family pets as a sign of his power, a threat of violence toward the family, or simply as an act of cruelty.

USE OF PRIVILEGE

The abuser will use whatever leverage he has against the victim, including social status, financial status, male privilege, race privilege, immigration status, and knowledge of the victim's personal information, such as gender identity, sexual orientation, or religious status. This may take the form of emotional or psychological abuse, with name-calling, demeaning, or degrading the victim based on status or lack of privilege. Male privilege may include using rigid sex roles as a means of control, such as demanding sex as a marital right. In LGBTQIA+ relationships, there may be threats to out the victim to friends, family, or colleagues. Where the victim is undocumented or not a US citizen, there may be threats to report the victim to US Immigration and Customs Enforcement (ICE) or other authorities.

II. Types of Abuse and Their Effects

The following is adapted from "Understanding Domestic Violence," an unpublished PowerPoint presentation by Dorchen Leidholdt, Esq., and Ted McCourtney, MSW.

Types of Abuse

PHYSICAL ABUSE

- Hitting, slapping, shoving, grabbing, pinching, biting, and pulling hair
- Choking you or trying to suffocate you
- Preventing access to medical care
- Having easy access to weapons
- Forcing you to use alcohol or drugs
- Driving dangerously while you are in the car

SEXUAL ABUSE

- Holding you down during sex
- Forcing you to have sex or making you do other sexual acts unwillingly
- Forcing you to have sex after hurting you or when you are sick or tired
- Calling you sexual names or forcing you to dress in a certain way
- Assaulting your genital area or breasts
- Pressuring/demanding that you have sex with other people
- Forcing you to watch or act out pornography
- Taking sexual/pornographic photographs of you and using them to manipulate your behavior, such as threatening to release them to friends and family or post them online

EMOTIONAL ABUSE

- Name-calling or insulting you
- Acting jealous and not trusting you
- Humiliating you
- Making you question your perception of reality within a relationship using statements like "That never happened" or "It's all in your head" (aka "gaslighting")
- Cheating on you repeatedly and then blaming you for the infidelity
- Damaging your relationships with your children

ECONOMIC ABUSE

- Withholding access to your money
- Refusing to let you go to work or school
- Forcing you to mount up debt to hurt your credit
- Refusing you access to money for necessities such as food and medical care
- Preventing you from viewing bank accounts
- Signing your name on financial instruments, such as rent, mortgages, car loans, etc., without your knowledge or against your will
- Allowing you to work but confiscating your paycheck
- Giving you a limited budget and forcing you to account for every penny spent

PSYCHOLOGICAL ABUSE

- Intimidating you
- Isolating you from other people
- Threatening to harm people you care about or pets
- Threatening to take your children
- Stalking you: following; sending unsolicited letters, messages, and/or gifts; destroying or vandalizing your property; threatening to harm your family members or friends
- Controlling your reproductive freedom by forcing sex, denying you access to contraceptives or abortion

DIGITAL ABUSE

- Controlling your passwords
- Searching your phone often, including texts and calls
- Monitoring you with any technology, such as a GPS
- Insulting you in social media status updates
- Engaging in cyber sexual abuse (also known as "revenge porn")
- Spoofing (setting up a false online profile of you intended to destroy your reputation)
- Installing spyware on your devices to intercept communication and personal information

- Sending defamatory messages about you through email and/ or social networking websites

LEGAL ABUSE

- Falsely reporting you to law enforcement or child welfare agencies
- Threatening deportation
- Initiating retaliatory cases, such as filing orders of protection, suing for custody, and making frivolous claims
- After the relationship has ended, gaining access to you by engaging in litigation
- Instituting legal proceedings that you cannot afford to fight

Effects of Abuse

PHYSICAL EFFECTS

- Direct physical injury: bruises, broken bones, lacerations, traumatic brain injury, vision and hearing impairment, damage to or loss of teeth
- Other physical effects: chronic headaches, pervasive body aches, feelings of dizziness
- Insomnia and disrupted or abnormal sleep
- Long-term physical effects: chronic illnesses such as heart disease (in middle- and old-age survivors), diabetes, autoimmune disorders, and stroke

PSYCHOLOGICAL EFFECTS

- High levels of anxiety
- Depression
- Minimization/denial
- Numbness/flattened affect
- Memory loss
- Dissociation
- Shame, self-blame
- Self-medication (drug/alcohol abuse)

- Post-traumatic stress disorder (PTSD)
- Intrusion: emotional reactions, flashbacks, images, nightmares
- Avoidance: dissociation, minimizing, numbing, denial
- Arousal: anger, difficulty concentrating or sleeping

LETHALITY INDICATORS

- Increase in severity or frequency of violence
- Use of or threats to use weapons
- Threats to kill you, children, and/or self
- Abuse of drugs or alcohol
- Stalking, choking, or forced sex
- Unemployment
- Separation

III. Resources

Whether you are a victim or a loved one seeking to support a victim, there are organizations you can turn to for help and information. What follows is a range of national and community-specific options. Several of the national organizations listed here include state-specific resources.

Resources for Immediate Safety Assistance

NATIONAL DOMESTIC VIOLENCE HOTLINE

https://www.thehotline.org
National Domestic Violence Hotline
P.O. Box 161810
Austin, TX 78716
1-800-799-7233

"Operating around the clock, seven days a week, confidential and free of cost, the National Domestic Violence Hotline provides life-saving tools and immediate support to enable victims to find safety and live lives free of abuse."

RAINN (RAPE, ABUSE AND INCEST NATIONAL NETWORK)

https://www.rainn.org

"RAINN (Rape, Abuse & Incest National Network) is the nation's largest anti–sexual violence organization. RAINN created and operates the National Sexual Assault Hotline (800-656-HOPE, online .rainn.org y rainn.org/es) in partnership with more than 1,000 local sexual assault service providers across the country and operates the DoD Safe Helpline for the Department of Defense. RAINN also carries out programs to prevent sexual violence, help survivors, and ensure that perpetrators are brought to justice."

FAMILY JUSTICE CENTER ALLIANCE

https://www.familyjusticecenter.org/affiliated-centers

"The Family Justice Center Alliance, a program of Alliance for HOPE International, is honored to support formally affiliated Family Justice Centers and Multi-Agency Centers across the United States. Affiliated Centers have demonstrated their commitment to the Guiding Principles of the Family Justice Center movement, a close working relationship with our national technical assistance and training program, and a focus on providing trauma-informed care for survivors and their children."

Family Justice Centers are designed to provide "one-stop shopping" for victims, including assistance with shelter, counseling, legal, and other services. Most are designed as walk-in centers that can be accessed by any victim in need. The link given here provides information about centers located throughout the United States.

Legal Resources

WOMENSLAW

https://www.womenslaw.org

"WomensLaw.org provides information that is relevant to people of all genders, not just women. Our Email Hotline will provide legal information to anyone who reaches out with legal questions or concerns regarding domestic violence, sexual violence, or any other topic covered on WomensLaw.org."

Also see the Family Justice Center Alliance.

AMERICAN BAR ASSOCIATION COMMISSION ON DOMESTIC AND SEXUAL VIOLENCE

https://www.americanbar.org/groups/domestic_violence
"Our mission is to increase access to justice for victims of domestic violence, sexual assault and stalking by mobilizing the legal profession. The ABA Commission on Domestic & Sexual Violence provides individualized support to attorneys representing victims of domestic violence, sexual assault and stalking, including research assistance, sample practice tools, model pleadings, and access to experts in the field."

TIME'S UP LEGAL DEFENSE FUND

https://nwlc.org/times-up-legal-defense-fund
legalnetwork@nwlc.org
"The TIME'S UP Legal Defense Fund, which is housed at and administered by the National Women's Law Center Fund LLC, a subsidiary of NWLC, connects those who experience sexual misconduct including assault, harassment, abuse and related retaliation in the workplace or in trying to advance their careers with legal and public relations assistance. The Fund will help defray legal and public relations costs in select cases based on criteria and availability of funds."

NATIONAL INSTITUTE OF JUSTICE (NIJ)

https://www.nij.gov/topics/crime/violence-against-women/pages/welcome.aspx
"The mission of the Violence Against Women and Family Violence Research and Evaluation program is to promote the safety of women and family members, and to increase the efficiency and effective-

ness of the criminal justice system's response to these crimes. This mission is being accomplished through estimating the scope of the problem to understand the extent of violence against women and family members, identifying causes and consequences to identify the reasons violent behavior against women and within the family occur, and evaluating promising prevention and intervention programs."

Community-Specific Resources

DAYA

> https://www.dayahouston.org
> Daya, Inc.
> P.O. Box 770773
> Houston, TX 77215
> Helpline: 1-713-981-7645
> Office: 1-713-842-7222

"Daya empowers South Asian survivors of domestic and sexual violence through culturally specific services and educates the community to end the cycle of abuse."

NATIONAL COALITION OF ANTI-VIOLENCE PROGRAMS (NCAVP)

> https://avp.org/ncavp
> National Coalition of Anti-Violence Programs
> 116 Nassau Street, 3rd floor
> New York, NY 10038
> 24-hour Bilingual Hotline: 1-212-714-1141
> Office: 1-212-714-1184

"We work to prevent, respond to, and end all forms of violence against and within LGBTQ communities. We're a national coalition of local member programs, affiliate organizations and individual affiliates who create systemic and social change. We strive to increase power, safety and resources through data analysis, policy advocacy, education and technical assistance."

NATIONAL INDIGENOUS WOMEN'S RESOURCE CENTER

http://www.niwrc.org
National Indigenous Women's Resource Center
515 Lame Deer Avenue
Lame Deer, MT 59043
1-406-477-3896

"The National Indigenous Women's Resource Center, Inc. (NIWRC) is a Native nonprofit organization that was created specifically to serve as the National Indian Resource Center (NIRC) Addressing Domestic Violence and Safety for Indian Women."

UJIMA, INC.: THE NATIONAL CENTER ON VIOLENCE AGAINST WOMEN IN THE BLACK COMMUNITY

https://ujimacommunity.org
1-844-77-UJIMA (85462)

"The mission of the National Center on Violence Against Women in the Black Community is to mobilize the community to respond to and end domestic, sexual and community violence in the Black community."

CASA DE ESPERANZA

https://casadeesperanza.org
Casa de Esperanza
P.O. Box 40115
St. Paul, MN 55104
24-hour Minnesota Crisis Line: 1-651-772-1611
24-hour National DV Hotline: 1-800-799-7233
Office: 1-651-646-5553
Email: info@casadeesperanza.org

"Casa de Esperanza is a leader in the domestic violence movement and a national resource center for organizations working with Latinas in the United States. Based in St. Paul, Minnesota, Casa de Esperanza's mission is to 'mobilize Latinas and Latin@ communities to end domestic violence.' Founded in 1982 to provide emergency shelter for Latinas and other women and children experiencing domestic violence, the organization has grown to become the largest Latina organization in the country focused on domestic violence. Casa de Esperanza is also committed to becoming a greater resource to organizations and communities in the areas of sexual assault and trafficking."

ASIAN PACIFIC ISLANDER DOMESTIC VIOLENCE RESOURCE PROJECT

> https://dvrp.org
> A/PI DVRP
> P.O. Box 14268
> Washington, DC 20044
> Hotline: 1-202-833-2233
> Office: 1-202-833-2232
> Email: info@dvrp.org

"The Asian/Pacific Islander Domestic Violence Resource Project (DVRP) is a non-profit organization in Washington, DC. Our mission is to address, prevent, and end domestic violence and sexual assault in Asian/Pacific Islander communities while empowering survivors to rebuild their lives after abuse."

DAY ONE

> https://www.dayoneny.org
> P.O. Box 3220
> Church Street Station
> New York, NY 10008
> Email: info@dayoneny.org
> Toll-Free Hotline: 1-800-214-4150
> Text Line: 1-646-535-DAY1 (3291)

Day One's mission is "to partner with youth to end dating abuse and domestic violence through community education, supportive services, legal advocacy and leadership development."

National Resources

NATIONAL COALITION AGAINST DOMESTIC VIOLENCE (NCADV)

http://www.ncadv.org
NCADV
One Broadway, Suite B210
Denver, CO 80203
1-303-839-1852

"The National Coalition Against Domestic Violence (NCADV)'s mission is to lead, mobilize and raise our voices to support efforts that demand a change of conditions that lead to domestic violence such as patriarchy, privilege, racism, sexism, and classism. We are dedicated to supporting survivors and holding offenders accountable and supporting advocates."

NATIONAL NETWORK TO END DOMESTIC VIOLENCE (NNEDV)

https://nnedv.org
National Network to End Domestic Violence
1325 Massachusetts Avenue NW, 7th Floor
Washington, DC 20005
1-202-543-5566

"The National Network to End Domestic Violence (NNEDV), a social change organization, is dedicated to creating a social, political, and economic environment in which violence against women no longer exists."

Trafficking

THE POLARIS PROJECT

https://polarisproject.org/get-assistance/national-human
-trafficking-hotline
The Polaris Project
P.O. Box 65323

Washington, DC 20035
1-202-790-6300
24-hour Hotline: 1-888-373-7888

"Founded in 2002, Polaris is named for the North Star, which people held in slavery in the United States used as a guide to navigate their way toward freedom. Today we are filling in the roadmap for that journey and lighting the path ahead by serving victims and survivors through the 24/7 National Human Trafficking Hotline, building one of the largest public data sets on human trafficking in the United States, and enlisting law enforcement and other public and private-sector partners, moving those strategies into the real world to support survivors."

ACKNOWLEDGMENTS

Infinite thanks to:

My literary agent, Meg Thompson; editor, Libby Burton; and everyone at Henry Holt and Company, especially Hannah Campbell, Amy Einhorn, Carolyn O'Keefe, and Maggie Richards for their belief in this book.

David Remnick, Jane Mayer, Ronan Farrow, Jyoti Thottam, Marin Cogan, and Amelia Schonbek for the care they gave my story.

Julie Fink, Jennifer Friedman, Robbie Kaplan, Rachel Tuchman, Rita Glavin, Sharon Nelles, Dorchen Leidholdt, and Wilder Knight for their counsel and guidance.

Arthur Bradford, Jenny Davidson, Mark Epstein, Catherine Gund, Cindi Leive, Larissa MacFarquhar, Elliot Thomson, and Kate Valk for their feedback on the manuscript.

Béatrice de Géa, KK Ottesen, and Damon Winter for their photographs. Ciara Alfaro, Clare Frucht, and Jillian Mannarino for research assistance.

All my family, friends, and colleagues for their support and insights as I wrote this book, including Laurie Anderson, Frank Andrews, Chloe Aridjis, Eva Aridjis, De'Ara Balenger,

Samantha Barry, Elizabeth Bawol, Mikaela Beardsley, Ginia Belafonte, Jennie Boddy, Jennifer Braunschweiger, Nell Breyer, Isolde Brielmaier, Winsome Brown, Heather Carlucci, Melissa Ceria, Julia Chaplin, Elaine Chen, Farai Chideya, Gabri Christa, Marsha Cooke, Lisa Cortés, Sue Craig, Amy Davidson, Celine DeCarlo, Joy de Menil, Sonali Deraniyagala, Nicolette Donen, Sarah Dougher, Geralyn White Dreyfous, Sandi DuBowski, Sarah Ellison, Wendy Ettinger, John Fleck, Sarah Sophie Flicker, China Forbes, Shari Frilot, CJ Frogozo, Shruti Ganguly, Caryn Ganz, Liz Garbus, Jennifer Gonnerman, Eric Gottesman, Leah Greenblatt, Vanessa Grigoriadis, Agnes Gund, Sol Guy, Dan Harris, Mara Hoffman, Hillary Jordan, Sibyl Kempson, Rachna Khare, Kim Krans, Sarah Lash, Thomas Lauderdale, Sarah Lewis, Lauren Lumsden, Alex and Vida Marashian, Elizabeth Cronise McLaughlin, Suketu Mehta, Elizabeth Méndez Berry, Liz Mermin, Laura Michalchyshyn, Sia Michel, Tim Miller, Debbie Millman, Unjoo Moon, Walter Mosley, Wendy Naugle, Hunter Noack, Emily Oberman, Andrew Ondrejcak, Sherwin Parikh, Lindsay Pera, Gabriela Poma, Alissa Quart, Linda Rattner, Amy Richards, Hannah Rosenzweig, Melena Ryzik, Wendy Sachs, Miguel Sancho, Gina Sanders, Therese Selvaratnam, Troy Selvaratnam, Danzy Senna, Wendy Shanker, Fiona Shaw, Meredith Shepherd, Tiffany Shlain, Heidi Sieck, Melissa Silverstein, Mark Skidmore, Mary Skinner, Andrew Solomon, Amy Lou Stein, Hank Willis Thomas, Lucy Walker, Kristina Wallison, Tamara Warren, Carrie Mae Weems, and Soon-Young Yoon.

The women who came forward with me; the women and men who have come forward with their stories; and the journalists and writers who have shown that, taking a cue from Naomi Alderman, we can understand our strength all at once.

NOTES

INTRODUCTION

3 In one year, this equates to: "National Statistics," National Coalition Against Domestic Violence, accessed October 7, 2019, https://ncadv .org/statistics.

3 "I feel that one of the strongest pathways": Leah Fessler, "Tarana Burke, Creator of Me Too, Believes You Don't Have to Sacrifice Everything for a Cause," *Quartz*, February 6, 2018, https://qz.com/work /1193569/me-too-movement-creator-tarana-burke-says-you-dont -have-to-sacrifice-everything-for-a-cause.

CHAPTER 1: THE FAIRY TALE

8 "the man the banks fear most": Harold Myerson, "The Man the Banks Fear Most," *The American Prospect*, April 23, 2012, https://prospect .org/api/amp/power/man-banks-fear.

8 "transforming the liberal checklist": Eric Schneiderman, "Transforming the Liberal Checklist," *The Nation*, February 21, 2008, https:// www.thenation.com/article/transforming-liberal-checklist.

CHAPTER 2: ENTRAP

20 "too much closeness terrifies": Beverly Engel, *The Emotionally Abusive Relationship: How to Stop Being Abused and How to Stop Abusing* (Hoboken, NJ: John Wiley and Sons, Inc., 2002), 204–5.

CHAPTER 4: CONTROL

33 "Control and dominance seem to give": Patricia Evans, *The Verbally Abusive Relationship: How to Recognize It and How to Respond* (New York: Adams Media, 2010), 40.

40 "the Dear Reader for whom every writer writes": Margaret Atwood, *The Handmaid's Tale* (New York: Anchor Books, 1986), xviii.

42 "By the time we met, the weight": Erika Harwood, "Sally Field Shares Details from Her Controlling Relationship with Burt Reynolds," *Vanity Fair*, September 18, 2018, https://www.vanityfair.com/style/2018/09/sally-field-memoir-burt-reynolds-relationship.

CHAPTER 5: DEMEAN

45 "while also trying to deflect the shade": Eileen Hoenigman Meyer, "How to Deal When a Colleague Is Threatened by You," *Glassdoor*, May 11, 2018, https://www.glassdoor.com/blog/threatened.

46 "To make contemporary women their personal property": Evan Stark, *Coercive Control: How Men Entrap Women in Personal Life* (New York: Oxford University Press, 2007), 197.

46 "any nonphysical behavior [or attitude]": Engel, *The Emotionally Abusive Relationship*, 10–11.

47 "Verbal abuse consistently discounts": Evans, *The Verbally Abusive Relationship*, 21.

47 "When these power plays are enacted": Evans, 21.

50 "Public speaking phobia has many causes": Susan Cain, *Quiet: The Power of Introverts in a World That Can't Stop Talking* (New York: Random House, 2013), 107.

51 "The truth is, few people put up with": Engel, *The Emotionally Abusive Relationship*, 58.

51 She also argues that women tend to hold: Engel, 76.

52 "Without an 'audience' for their victimization": Stark, *Coercive Control*, 110.

CHAPTER 6: ABUSE

53 "the dynamics that lie behind the intense": Susan Weitzman, *"Not to People Like Us": Hidden Abuse in Upscale Marriages* (New York: Basic Books, 2000), 24.

53 isolation "is then fueled by the very real fear": Weitzman, *"Not to People Like Us,"* 34.

54 "Every twelve seconds a woman suffers": Weitzman, 4.

57 "ten percent of women report quitting": Elizabeth Méndez Berry, "Street Harassment: The Uncomfortable Walk Home," *Crunk Feminist Collective*, September 16, 2010, https://www.crunkfeministcollective .com/2010/09/16/street-harassment-the-uncomfortable-walk -home.

57 "Arousal and orgasm are no longer": Atwood, *The Handmaid's Tale*, 94.

59 "We may be more likely to make things worse": Sarah Schulman, *Conflict Is Not Abuse: Overstating Harm, Community Responsibility, and the Duty of Repair* (Vancouver, Canada: Arsenal Pulp Press, 2016), 191.

60 "essentially a junk drawer of disconnected symptoms": David J. Morris, *The Evil Hours: A Biography of Post-Traumatic Stress Disorder* (New York: Eamon Dolan Books, 2015), 13–14.

61 "Speaking more gently, listening more attentively": Evans, *The Verbally Abusive Relationship*, 101–2.

63 "There were many reasons I wanted to be with him": Megan McArdle, "I Went Back to a Man Who Hit Me. I'm Still Thinking About Why," *Washington Post*, May 8, 2018, https://www.washingtonpost .com/opinions/i-went-back-to-the-man-who-hit-me-why/2018/05 /08/0acb4c54-52f2-11e8-abd8-265bd07a9859_story.html.

CHAPTER 7: THE NIGHTMARE

66 "It always has your best interest at heart": Gavin de Becker, *The Gift of Fear: And Other Survival Signals That Protect Us from Violence* (New York: Dell Publishing, 1997), 71.

70 Megan Twohey wrote: Megan Twohey, "Tumult After AIDS Fundraiser Supports Harvey Weinstein Production," *New York Times*, September 23, 2017, https://www.nytimes.com/2017/09/23/nyregion/ harvey-weinstein-charity.html.

70 "Inside Harvey Weinstein's Other Nightmare": William D. Cohan, "'Nothing About This Deal Seems Right to Me': Inside Harvey Weinstein's Other Nightmare," *Vanity Fair*, December 20, 2017, https:// www.vanityfair.com/news/2017/12/harvey-weinstein-nightmare -finding-neverland-amfar-money.

70 Soon thereafter, internet searches for "complicit": Amy B. Wang, "'Complicit' Is the 2017 Word of the Year, According to Dictionary.com," *Washington Post*, November 27, 2017, https://www.washingtonpost .com/news/the-intersect/wp/2017/11/27/complicit-is-the-2017 -word-of-the-year-according-to-dictionary-com.

72 "I wanted him to see me as an artist": Salma Hayek, "Harvey Weinstein Is My Monster Too," *New York Times*, December 12, 2017, https://www.nytimes.com/interactive/2017/12/13/opinion/contributors/salma-hayek-harvey-weinstein.html.

72 "[Physical abuse] is most often hidden from even": Rachel Louise Snyder, *No Visible Bruises: What We Don't Know About Domestic Violence Can Kill Us* (New York: Bloomsbury Publishing, 2019), 10.

73 "the first stage of recognition is the beginning": Evans, *The Verbally Abusive Relationship*, 113.

74 In 2018, the W. M. Keck Center: Emma M. Millon, Han Yan M. Chang, and Tracy J. Shors, "Stressful Life Memories Relate to Ruminative Thoughts in Women with Sexual Violence History, Irrespective of PTSD," *Frontiers in Psychiatry*, September 5, 2018, https://www.frontiersin.org/articles/10.3389/fpsyt.2018.00311/full.

74 "Victims of sexual violence reported 44%": Jessica Ravitz and Arman Azad, "Memories That Last: What Sexual Assault Survivors Remember and Why," *CNN*, September 21, 2018, https://www.cnn.com/2018/09/21/health/memory-sexual-assault-ptsd/index.html.

74 "Bill Cosby took my beautiful, healthy young spirit": Ron Allen and Daniel Arkin, "Bill Cosby Accusers Cry, Rejoice After He Is Sentenced to Prison Time," *NBC News*, September 25, 2018, https://www.nbcnews.com/storyline/bill-cosby-%20%20scandal/bill-cosby-accusers-cry-rejoice-after-he-sentenced-prison-time-n913086.

CHAPTER 8: WHAT IS INTIMATE VIOLENCE?

77 "Research suggests that physical violence": World Health Organization, "Violence by Intimate Partners," in *World Report on Violence and Health*, eds. Etienne G. Krug, Linda L. Dahlberg, James A. Mercy, Anthony B. Zwi, and Rafael Lozano (Geneva: World Health Organization, 2002), http://www.who.int/violence_injury_prevention/violence/global_campaign/en/chap4.pdf.

78 "patriarchy is . . . the structurally induced hatred of women": Brittney C. Cooper, *Eloquent Rage: A Black Feminist Discovers Her Superpower* (New York: Picador, 2018), 91.

78 and 76.8 percent of aggravated assaults: Federal Bureau of Investigation, "Table 33: Ten-Year Arrest Trends," FBI: Uniform Crime Reporting, accessed October 7, 2019, https://ucr.fbi.gov/crime-in-the-u.s/2017/crime-in-the-u.s.-2017/topic-pages/tables/table-33.

78 almost 30 percent . . . have experienced intimate partner violence:

World Health Organization, *WHO: Addressing Violence Against Women: Key Achievements and Priorities* (Geneva: World Health Organization, 2018), http://apps.who.int/iris/bitstream/handle /10665/275982/WHO-RHR-18.18-eng.pdf?ua=1.

79 Community and societal factors: Claudia Garcia-Moreno, Alessandra Guedes, and Wendy Knerr, "Intimate Partner Violence," in *Understanding and Addressing Violence Against Women*, ed. Sarah Ramsay (Geneva: World Health Organization, 2012), http://apps.who.int/iris /bitstream/10665/77432/1/WHO_RHR_12.36_eng.pdf.

82 Jane Mayer has written about . . . Al Franken: Jane Mayer, "The Case of Al Franken," *New Yorker*, July 22, 2019, https://www.newyorker.com /magazine/2019/07/29/the-case-of-al-franken.

83 I knew McIntosh but became aware: Jess McIntosh, "I Went on a Date with Eric Schneiderman. It Took Me Years to Process What Happened That Night," *Elle*, May 31, 2018, https://www.elle.com/culture /a20896599/eric-schneiderman-date-story-jess-mcintosh.

84 Of the one in fifteen children exposed: "National Statistics," National Coalition Against Domestic Violence, accessed October 7, 2019, https://ncadv.org/statistics.

85 It meant that she forgave the world: "Get to Know Sharon White-Harrigan, Prison Reform Activist," Makers.com, video, 4:49, accessed October 7, 2019, https://www.makers.com/profiles /5c5ca6cf14925a51091530c2.

86 David Remnick, in a *New Yorker* article: David Remnick, "The Weinstein Moment and the Trump Presidency," *New Yorker*, November 20, 2017, https://www.newyorker.com/magazine/2017/11/20/the -weinstein-moment-and-the-trump-presidency.

87 In a February 2018 article for the *Guardian*: Jessica Valenti, "Why Domestic Abusers Thrive in Trump's White House," *Guardian*, February 9, 2018, https://www.theguardian.com/commentisfree/2018 /feb/09/why-domestic-abusers-trump-white-house.

88 an American was sexually assaulted: RAINN (Rape, Abuse, Incest National Network): "Scope of the Problem: Statistics," RAINN, accessed October 7, 2019, https://www.rainn.org/statistics/scope -problem.

88 epidemic of "Hazing, Humiliation, Terror" for female workers in prisons: Caitlin Dickerson, "Hazing, Humiliation, Terror: Working While Female in Federal Prison," *New York Times*, November 17, 2018, https://www.nytimes.com/2018/11/17/us/prison-sexual -harassment-women.html.

89 "everyone . . . saw the video of me naked": Lauren Katzenberg, "40 Stories from Women About Life in the Military," *New York Times*, March 8, 2019, https://www.nytimes.com/2019/03/08/magazine/women-military-stories.html.

89 she "felt like the system was raping [her] all over again": Emily Cochrane and Jennifer Steinhauer, "Senator Martha McSally Says Superior Officer in the Air Force Raped Her," *New York Times*, March 6, 2019, https://www.nytimes.com/2019/03/06/us/politics/martha-mcsally-sexual-assault.html.

90 "more than 100 documented reports": Manny Fernandez, "'You Have to Pay with Your Body': The Hidden Nightmare of Sexual Violence on the Border," *New York Times*, March 3, 2019, https://www.nytimes.com/2019/03/03/us/border-rapes-migrant-women.html.

90 "Forty-seven percent of transgender people report": Stephanie Zacharek, Eliana Dockterman, and Haley Sweetland Edwards, "The Silence Breakers," *Time*, December 6, 2017, http://time.com/time-person-of-the-year-2017-silence-breakers.

90 the CDC has declared same-sex domestic violence an epidemic: Maya Shwayder, "A Same-Sex Violence Epidemic Is Silent," *Atlantic*, November 5, 2013, https://www.theatlantic.com/health/archive/2013/11/a-same-sex-domestic-violence-epidemic-is-silent/281131.

90 Intimate partner violence . . . negative health outcomes: World Health Organization, *Addressing Violence Against Women*.

91 "Intimate partner violence costs women": Snyder, *No Visible Bruises*, 122.

91 "Sexual violence is . . . an assault against the blood": "'An Indigenous Response to #MeToo'—Is an Engaging Conversation Starter to Break the Silence and Lean Into Cultural Teachings for Viable Solutions," *Native News Online*, April 5, 2018, https://nativenewsonline.net/currents/an-indigenous-response-to-metoo-is-an-engaging-conversation-starter-to-break-the-silence-and-lean-into-cultural-teachings-for-viable-solutions.

CHAPTER 9: EXTRACTION

98 that 63 percent of homeless women: Soraya Chemaly, *Rage Becomes Her: The Power of Women's Anger* (New York: Atria Books, 2019), 149.

CHAPTER 10: THE PATTERN

106 "Dr. Johnnie Barto used his position": Corky Siemaszko, "For Decades, a Sexual Predator Doctor Groomed This Community to Believe He Could Do No Wrong," *NBC News*, March 17, 2019, https://www

.nbcnews.com/news/us-news/decades-sexual-predator-doctor
-groomed-community-believe-he-could-do-n982131.

113 "New York's Attorney General in Battle with Trump": Danny Hakim
and William K. Rosenbaum, "New York's Attorney General in Battle
with Trump," *New York Times*, December 26, 2017, https://www
.nytimes.com/2017/12/26/nyregion/eric-schneiderman-attorney
-general-new-york.html.

113 "What It Takes to Keep Trump in Check:" Ben Schreckinger, "New
York Attorney General Eric Schneiderman on What It Takes to
Keep Trump in Check," *GQ*, November 29, 2017, https://www.gq
.com/story/new-york-attorney-general-eric-schneiderman-trump
-interview.

115 "More and more now I keep my balance": Sonali Deraniyagala, *Wave*
(New York: Alfred A. Knopf, 2013), 226.

115 "To withhold words is power. But to share our words with others,
openly and honestly, is also power": Terry Tempest Williams, *When
Women Were Birds: Fifty-four Variations on Voice* (New York: Picador,
2012), 16.

CHAPTER 11: COMING FORWARD

124 "a man who could be both charming and romantic": Andrew Prokop,
"The Rob Porter Scandal Keeps Getting Worse for Trump's White
House," *Vox*, February 9, 2018, https://www.vox.com/policy-and
-politics/2018/2/8/16988560/rob-porter-allegations-resigns.

124 "Rob Porter's History of Domestic Abuse Wasn't": Dahlia Lithwick,
"Rob Porter's History of Domestic Abuse Wasn't a Secret. It's Just
That No One Cared," *Slate*, February 8, 2018, https://slate.com/news
-and-politics/2018/02/rob-porters-history-of-domestic-abuse-wasnt
-a-secret.html.

124 "Domestic violence in any form is abhorrent": Quoted in Lithwick,
"Rob Porter's History of Domestic Abuse Wasn't a Secret."

125 "His value outweighed her sexualized worthlessness": Catharine A.
MacKinnon, "#MeToo Has Done What the Law Could Not," *New
York Times*, February 4, 2018, https://www.nytimes.com/2018/02
/04/opinion/metoo-law-legal-system.html.

125 "Thankfully, my strength and worth": Jennie Willoughby, "Jennie Willoughby: 'President Trump Will Not Diminish My Truth,'" *Time*, February 11, 2018, http://time.com/5143589/rob-porter-ex-wife-trump
-domestic-violence.

127 "He spoke at a lectern with the words": Andrew Ross Sorkin, "Does

a Lawsuit Now Help the Weinstein Victims?," *New York Times*, February 12, 2018, https://www.nytimes.com/2018/02/12/business/dealbook/weinstein-victims-lawsuit.html.

CHAPTER 12: THE ROLLER COASTER

137 Eighty-five percent said that they "believe": Zacharek, Dockterman, and Edwards, "The Silence Breakers."

CHAPTER 13: THE FALLOUT

148 "I therefore resign my office": Aaron Katersky, Josh Margolin, and Justin Doom, "NY Attorney General Eric Schneiderman Resigns After Report He Abused 4 Women," *ABC News*, May 8, 2018, https://abcnews.go.com/Politics/york-attorney-general-resign-reports-abuse-women/story?id=55002677.

149 "I find it impossible to believe these allegations": Ronan Farrow and Jane Mayer, "Four Women Accuse New York's Attorney General of Physical Abuse," *New Yorker*, May 7, 2018, https://www.newyorker.com/news/news-desk/four-women-accuse-new-yorks-attorney-general-of-physical-abuse.

151 "Christiane Amanpour . . . interviewing Barbara Underwood": Rebecca Traister, *Good and Mad: The Revolutionary Power of Women's Anger* (New York: Simon and Schuster, 2019), 219.

152 "Eric Schneiderman and Men Who Excuse": Madeleine Aggeler, "Eric Schneiderman and Men Who Excuse Violence As 'Kink,'" *The Cut*, May 8, 2018, https://www.thecut.com/2018/05/eric-schneiderman-sexual-assault-kink-bdsm.html.

152 "Here's How Consent and BDSM Role-Play": Alexa Tsoulis-Reay, "Here's How Consent and BDSM Role-Play Actually Work," *The Cut*, May 9, 2018, https://www.thecut.com/2018/05/how-to-role-play-bdsm-for-beginners.html.

154 "[S]he had unintentionally been less than honest": Carolyn G. Heilbrun, *Writing a Woman's Life* (New York: W. W. Norton and Company, Inc., 1988), 12–13.

155 According to the *New York Times*, Gleason: Alan Feuer, "Lawyer for 2 Schneiderman Accusers Brought Their Claims to Michael Cohen," *New York Times*, May 11, 2018, https://www.nytimes.com/2018/05/11/nyregion/eric-schneiderman-michael-cohen.html.

158 I'd made it onto *The Daily Show*: Trevor Noah, "Eric 'Champion of Women' Schneiderman Falls to Me Too Movement," Comedy Central, May 8, 2018, video, 5:22, http://www.cc.com/video-clips

/930keb/the-daily-show-with-trevor-noah-eric—champion-of
-women—schneiderman-falls-to-the-me-too-movement.

160 Samantha Bee spoke with Rebecca Traister: *Vulture* Editors, "Samantha Bee and the *Full Frontal* Team Reflect on Their Wild Ride Since
the Election," *Vulture*, August 24, 2018, http://www.vulture.com
/2018/08/samantha-bee-full-frontal-vulture-fest.html.

165 That big story was about . . . Les Moonves: Ronan Farrow, "As Leslie Moonves Negotiates His Exit from CBS, Six Women Raise New
Assault and Harassment Claims," *New Yorker*, September 9, 2018,
https://www.newyorker.com/news/news-desk/as-leslie-moonves
-negotiates-his-exit-from-cbs-women-raise-new-assault-and
-harassment-claims.

CHAPTER 14: THE LESSON

167 Forty-seven percent of white women voted: Molly Ball, "Donald
Trump Didn't Really Win 52% of White Women in 2016," *Time*,
October 18, 2018, https://time.com/5422644/trump-white-women
-2016.

168 "One year after Donald Trump had faced no repercussions": Traister,
Good and Mad, 38.

168 "Women are gonna take charge of society": Quoted in David Remnick, "A Reckoning with Women Awaits Trump," *New Yorker*, February 11, 2018, https://www.newyorker.com/news/daily-comment/a
-reckoning-with-women-awaits-trump.

170 a program called Becoming a Man (BAM): Andrew Reiner, "Boy
Talk: Breaking Masculine Stereotypes," *New York Times*, October 24,
2018, https://www.nytimes.com/2018/10/24/well/family/boy-talk
-breaking-masculine-stereotypes.html.

170 "conversations about what it means to be a man": Cooper, *Eloquent
Rage*, 92.

171 "You simply need to be very clear": Kwame Anthony Appiah, "Should
I Warn My Daughter About My Abusive Ex-Husband?," The Ethicist,
New York Times, April 16, 2019, https://www.nytimes.com/2019/04
/16/magazine/ethicist-abusive-ex-husband.html.

172 In June 2019, E. Jean Carroll: E. Jean Carroll, "Hideous Men: Donald
Trump Assaulted Me in a Bergdorf Goodman Dressing Room 23 Years
Ago. But He's Not Alone on the List of Awful Men in My Life," *The
Cut*, June 21, 2019, https://www.thecut.com/2019/06/donald-trump
-assault-e-jean-carroll-other-hideous-men.html.

172 "This dynamic is central to both": Jia Tolentino, "E. Jean Carroll's

Accusation Against Donald Trump, and the Raising, and Lowering, of the Bar," *New Yorker*, June 25, 2019, https://www.newyorker.com /news/our-columnists/e-jean-carrolls-accusation-against-donald -trump-and-the-raising-and-lowering-of-the-bar.

173 "But it can also be powerful, inspiring, fun": Cecile Richards, *Make Trouble: Stand Up, Speak Out, and Find the Courage to Lead* (New York: Simon and Schuster, 2018), xi.

173 "But the lasting legacy of this moment": Richards, *Make Trouble*, 257.

173 "What fresh hell awaits us in tomorrow's news?": Richard Morgan, "Ken Friedman, Spotted Pig Owner, Steps Down After Sexual Harassment Accusations," *Time Out*, December 12, 2017, https:// www.timeout.com/newyork/news/ken-friedman-spotted-pig-owner -steps-down-after-sexual-harassment-accusations-121217.

174 "Forty-three percent of their replacements": Audrey Carlsen, Maya Salam, Claire Cain Miller, Denise Lu, Ash Ngu, Jugal K. Patel, and Zach Wichter, "#MeToo Brought Down 201 Powerful Men. Nearly Half of Their Replacements Are Women," *New York Times*, October 23, 2018, https://www.nytimes.com/interactive/2018/10/23/us /metoo-replacements.html.

174 "women now represent 46 percent of the parliament": Celestine Bohlen, "Sweden Provides Some Perspective on Women and Equality," *New York Times*, March 8, 2019, https://www.nytimes.com/2019/03 /08/world/europe/sweden-women-equal-representation.html.

175 "The early openings of the butterflies' wings": Catharine MacKinnon, "Where #MeToo Came From, and Where It's Going," *Atlantic*, March 24, 2019, https://www.theatlantic.com/ideas/archive/2019 /03/catharine-mackinnon-what-metoo-has-changed/585313.

175 "It's amazing that for the first time": Ariane de Vogue, "#MeToo Will Have Staying Power, Ruth Bader Ginsburg Insists," *CNN*, February 12, 2018, https://www.cnn.com/2018/02/11/politics/ruth-bader -ginsburg-me-too-poppy-harlow/index.html.

175 "I like to say I won": Editors of *The Cut*, "Anita Hill: Won, Even Though She Lost," *The Cut*, October 15, 2018, https://www.thecut .com/2018/10/women-and-power-chapter-one.html.

176 "On several occasions, Thomas told me graphically": Mikayla Bouchard and Marisa Schwartz Taylor, "Flashback: The Anita Hill Hearings Compared to Today," *New York Times*, September 27, 2018, https:// www.nytimes.com/2018/09/27/us/politics/anita-hill-kavanaugh -hearings.html.

176 "'The healing from sexual violence must begin now'": Anita Hill, "Anita Hill: Let's Talk About How to End Sexual Violence," *New York Times*, May 9, 2019, https://www.nytimes.com/2019/05/09/opinion/anita-hill-sexual-violence.html.

176 "To this day I regret I couldn't": Scott Bixby, "Clarence Thomas Accuser Sukari Hardnett Hopes Biden Learned from His 'Mistake,'" *Daily Beast*, March 29, 2019, https://www.thedailybeast.com/clarence-thomas-accuser-sukari-hardnett-hopes-biden-learned-from-his-mistake.

177 "somebody on the court who . . . lied under oath": Molly Langmuir, "What's Next for *New Yorker* Reporter Jane Mayer?," *Elle*, February 27, 2019, https://www.elle.com/culture/a26537529/jane-mayer-new-yorker-interview-kavanaugh.

177 "It failed on both counts": Anita Hill, "Anita Hill: How to Get the Kavanaugh Hearings Right," *New York Times*, September 18, 2018, https://www.nytimes.com/2018/09/18/opinion/anita-hill-brett-kavanaugh-clarence-thomas.html.

178 "It was hard for me to breathe": Dylan Scott, "Read Christine Blasey Ford's Written Testimony: 'I Am Here Today Not Because I Want to Be. I Am Terrified,'" *Vox*, September 27, 2018, https://www.vox.com/2018/9/26/17907462/christine-blasey-ford-testimony-brett-kavanaugh-hearing.

179 "The survey found . . . only fifty-four percent of Republicans": Zacharek, Dockterman, and Edwards, "The Silence Breakers."

179 "called for a special working group": Joan Biskupic, "Federal Courts Say They'll Now Track Sexual Harassment Data," *CNN*, February 20, 2018, https://www.cnn.com/2018/02/20/politics/courts-sexual-harassment-data/index.html.

179 "There is no place in the Academy": Rory Carroll, "Hollywood After Weinstein: 'The Animals Have No Choice but to Be Civilized,'" *Guardian*, January 1, 2018, https://www.theguardian.com/film/2018/jan/01/hollywood-sexual-misconduct-after-weinstein.

180 Another agency, WME, paid for: Dana Goodyear, "Can Hollywood Change Its Ways?," *New Yorker*, January 1, 2018, https://www.newyorker.com/magazine/2018/01/08/can-hollywood-change-its-ways.

180 "We must make it unequivocally clear": Itay Hod, "Anita Hill Calls on Hollywood to Make 'Tangible Commitments' to Address Harassment and Equality Goals," *The Wrap*, October 8, 2018, https://www.thewrap.com/anita-hill-calls-hollywood-make-tangible-commitments-address-harassment-equality-goals.

181 "'You're doing fine,' he assured me": Connie Chung, "Dear Christine Blasey Ford: I, Too, Was Sexually Assaulted—and It's Seared into My Memory Forever," *Washington Post*, October 3, 2018, https://www .washingtonpost.com/opinions/dear-christine-blasey-ford-i-too-was -sexually-assaulted—and-its-seared-into-my-memory-forever/2018 /10/03/2449ed3c-c68a-11e8-9b1c-a90f1daae309_story.html.

183 "assembling a large, cult-like network of underage girls": Julie K. Brown, "How a Future Trump Cabinet Member Gave a Serial Sex Abuser the Deal of a Lifetime," *Miami Herald*, November 28, 2018, https://www.miamiherald.com/news/local/article220097825.html.

183 "despite explicit sheriff's department rules": Brown, "How a Future Trump Cabinet Member."

183 "How in the world, do you, the U.S. attorney": Brown, "How a Future Trump Cabinet Member."

185 "many people who had never believed black girls' allegations": Salamishah Tillet and Scheherazade Tillet, "After the 'Surviving R. Kelly' Documentary, #MeToo Has Finally Returned to Black Girls," *New York Times*, February 2, 2019, https://www.nytimes.com/2019/01 /10/opinion/r-kelly-documentary-metoo.html.

185 "To everyone telling me how courageous I am": Quoted in Christina Maxouris, "R. Kelly Docuseries Leaves Behind a Burning Question: Do Black Girls' Lives Matter?," *CNN*, February 2, 2019, https://www .cnn.com/2019/01/07/entertainment/r-kelly-celebrities-react-on -docuseries/index.html.

186 "Something changed in me that year. It made me just not want to make music": Joe Coscarelli and Melena Ryzik, "Ryan Adams Dangled Success. Women Say They Paid a Price," *New York Times*, February 13, 2019, https://www.nytimes.com/2019/02/13/arts/music/ryan -adams-women-sex.html.

186 "He couldn't have done this without them": Jem Aswad, "Phoebe Bridgers Slams Ryan Adams's 'Network' of Enablers," *Variety*, February 17, 2019, https://variety.com/2019/music/news/phoebe-bridgers- slams-ryan-adams-network-of-enablers-1203141929.

187 "the conviction that they . . . are the real victims": Glenn Whipp, "A Year After #MeToo Upended the Status Quo, the Accused Are Attempting Comebacks—But Not Offering Apologies," *Los Angeles Times*, October 5, 2018, http://www.latimes.com/entertainment/la -ca-mn-me-too-men-apology-20181005-story.html.

187 In 2012, he undertook "a public relations campaign": Julie K. Brown,

"For Years, Jeffrey Epstein Abused Teen Girls, Police Say: A Time-line of His Case," *Miami Herald*, November 28, 2018, https://www.miamiherald.com/news/local/article221404845.html.

188 During the 2019 Sundance Film Festival: Trey Williams, "Former Weinstein Exec David Glasser Launches New 101 Studios," *The Wrap*, January 22, 2019, https://www.thewrap.com/former-weinstein-exec-david-glasser-launches-new-company-101-studios.

189 "'I am learning to feel respect for women'": Mary McNamara, "Must Reads: Emma Thompson's Letter to Skydance: Why I Can't Work for John Lasseter," *Los Angeles Times*, February 26, 2019, https://www.latimes.com/entertainment/la-et-mn-emma-thompson-john-lasseter-skydance-20190226-story.html.

189 Every time the teacher sees the girl: Naomi Alderman, *The Power* (New York: Little, Brown and Company, 2016), 123.

189 "Disturbingly, the requirement of 'intent'": Ginia Bellafante, "The #MeToo Movement Changed Everything. Can the Law Catch Up?," *New York Times*, November 21, 2018, https://www.nytimes.com/2018/11/21/nyregion/metoo-movement-schneiderman-prosecution.html.

190 "every Constitution in the world": de Vogue, "#MeToo Will Have Staying Power, Ruth Bader Ginsburg Insists."

190 "It could renovate interpretations of equality": MacKinnon, "Where #MeToo Came From, and Where It's Going."

190 But Title VII does not apply: Alieza Durana, "The Sexual-Harassment Victims Who Can't Get to Court," *Atlantic*, October 8, 2018, https://www.theatlantic.com/ideas/archive/2018/10/year-metoo-not-everyones-protected-sexual-harassment/572329.

191 "Providing support for interviewees": World Health Organization, "Violence by Intimate Partners," 92–93.

192 As a result, its nonattendance rate: World Health Organization, "Violence by Intimate Partners," 106.

193 His father had the indecency to say: Elle Hunt, "'20 Minutes of Action': Father Defends Stanford Student Son Convicted of Sexual Assault," *Guardian*, June 5, 2016, https://www.theguardian.com/us-news/2016/jun/06/father-stanford-university-student-brock-turner-sexual-assault-statement.

193 "Men learn to regard rape as a moment in time": Chemaly, *Rage Becomes Her*, 126.

193 "It is the holding of the secret": Kevin Fallon, "Oprah Takes a Powerful

Stand on 'Leaving Neverland' Controversy: 'This Moment Transcends Michael Jackson,'" *Daily Beast*, March 5, 2019, https://www.thedailybeast.com/oprah-takes-a-powerful-stand-on-leaving-neverland-controversy-this-moment-transcends-michael-jackson.

194 "you are powerful and nobody can": Katie J. M. Baker, "Here's the Powerful Letter the Stanford Victim Read to Her Attacker," *BuzzFeed News*, June 3, 2016, https://www.buzzfeednews.com/article/katiejmbaker/heres-the-powerful-letter-the-stanford-victim-read-to-her-ra.

194 Chanel Miller told her story: Chanel Miller, *Know My Name: A Memoir* (New York: Viking, 2019).

CHAPTER 15: MOVING FORWARD

199 "We understand our strength, all at once": Tanya Selvaratnam, "What Happened After I Shared My Story of Abuse by New York's Attorney General," *New York Times*, October 6, 2018, https://www.nytimes.com/2018/10/06/opinion/sunday/eric-schneiderman-abuse.html.

CODA (SIX MONTHS LATER)

204 "legal impediments, including statutes of limitations": Alan Feuer, "Schneiderman Will Not Face Criminal Charges in Abuse Complaints," *New York Times*, November 8, 2018, https://www.nytimes.com/2018/11/08/nyregion/eric-schneiderman-abuse-charges.html.

204 He also said that he had been seeking: Feuer, "Schneiderman Will Not Face Criminal Charges in Abuse Complaints."

BIBLIOGRAPHY

Aggeler, Madeleine. "Eric Schneiderman and Men Who Excuse Violence As 'Kink.'" *The Cut*, May 8, 2018. https://www.thecut.com/2018/05/eric-schneiderman-sexual-assault-kink-bdsm.html.

Alderman, Naomi. *The Power*. New York: Little, Brown and Company, 2016.

Allen, Ron, and Daniel Arkin. "Bill Cosby Accusers Cry, Rejoice After He Is Sentenced to Prison Time." NBC News, September 25, 2018. https://www.nbcnews.com/storyline/bill-cosby-%20%20scandal/bill-cosby-accusers-cry-rejoice-after-he-sentenced-prison-time-n913086.

Appiah, Kwame Anthony. "Should I Warn My Daughter About My Abusive Ex-Husband?" The Ethicist. *New York Times*, April 16, 2019. https://www.nytimes.com/2019/04/16/magazine/ethicist-abusive-ex-husband.html.

Aswad, Jem. "Phoebe Bridgers Slams Ryan Adams's 'Network' of Enablers." *Variety*, February 17, 2019. https://variety.com/2019/music/news/phoebe-bridgers-slams-ryan-adams-network-of-enablers-1203141929.

Atwood, Margaret. *The Handmaid's Tale*. New York: Anchor Books, 1986.

Baker, Katie J. M. "Here's the Powerful Letter the Stanford Victim Read to Her Attacker." *BuzzFeed News*, June 3, 2016. https://www.buzzfeednews.com/article/katiejmbaker/heres-the-powerful-letter-the-stanford-victim-read-to-her-ra.

Ball, Molly. "Donald Trump Didn't Really Win 52% of White Women in 2016." *Time*, October 18, 2018. https://time.com/5422644/trump-white-women-2016.

Bellafante, Ginia. "The #MeToo Movement Changed Everything. Can the Law Catch Up?" *New York Times*, November 21, 2018. https://www.nytimes.com/2018/11/21/nyregion/metoo-movement-schneiderman-prosecution.html.

Biskupic, Joan. "Courts Say They'll Now Track Sexual Harassment Data." *CNN*, February 20, 2018. https://www.cnn.com/2018/02/20/politics/courts-sexual-harassment-data/index.html.

Bixby, Scott. "Clarence Thomas Accuser Sukari Hardnett Hopes Biden Learned from His 'Mistake.'" *Daily Beast*, March 29, 2019. https://www.thedailybeast.com/clarence-thomas-accuser-sukari-hardnett-hopes-biden-learned-from-his-mistake.

Bohlen, Celestine. "Sweden Provides Some Perspective on Women and Equality." *New York Times*, March 8, 2019. https://www.nytimes.com/2019/03/08/world/europe/sweden-women-equal-representation.html.

Bouchard, Mikayla, and Marisa Schwartz Taylor. "Flashback: The Anita Hill Hearings Compared to Today." *New York Times*, September 27, 2018. https://www.nytimes.com/2018/09/27/us/politics/anita-hill-kavanaugh-hearings.html.

Brown, Julie K. "For Years, Jeffrey Epstein Abused Teen Girls, Police Say. A Timeline of His Case." *Miami Herald*, November 28, 2018. https://www.miamiherald.com/news/local/article221404845.html.

———. "How a Future Trump Cabinet Member Gave a Serial Sex Abuser the Deal of a Lifetime." *Miami Herald*, November 28, 2018. https://www.miamiherald.com/news/local/article220097825.html.

Cain, Susan. *Quiet: The Power of Introverts in a World That Can't Stop Talking*. New York: Random House, 2013.

Carlsen, Audrey, Maya Salam, Claire Cain Miller, Denise Lu, Ash Ngu, Jugal K. Patel, and Zach Wichter. "#MeToo Brought Down 201 Powerful Men. Nearly Half of Their Replacements Are Women." *New York Times*, October 23, 2018. https://www.nytimes.com/interactive/2018/10/23/us/metoo-replacements.html.

Carroll, E. Jean. "Hideous Men: Donald Trump Assaulted Me in a Bergdorf Goodman Dressing Room 23 Years Ago. But He's Not Alone on the List of Awful Men in My Life." *The Cut*, June 21, 2019. https://www.thecut.com/2019/06/donald-trump-assault-e-jean-carroll-other-hideous-men.html.

Carroll, Rory. "Hollywood After Weinstein: 'The Animals Have No Choice But to Be Civilized.'" *Guardian*, January 1, 2018. https://www.theguardian.com/film/2018/jan/01/hollywood-sexual-misconduct-after-weinstein.

Chemaly, Soraya. *Rage Becomes Her: The Power of Women's Anger*. New York: Atria Books, 2019.

Chung, Connie. "Dear Christine Blasey Ford: I, Too, Was Sexually Assaulted—and It's Seared into My Memory Forever." *Washington Post*, October 3, 2018. https://www.washingtonpost.com/opinions/dear-christine-blasey-ford-i-too-was-sexually-assaulted—and-its-seared-into-my-memory-forever/2018/10/03/2449ed3c-c68a-11e8-9b1c-a90f1daae309_story.html.

Cochrane, Emily, and Jennifer Steinhauer. "Senator Martha McSally Says Superior Officer in the Air Force Raped Her." *New York Times*, March 6, 2019. https://www.nytimes.com/2019/03/06/us/politics/martha-mcsally-sexual-assault.html.

Cohan, William D. "'Nothing About This Deal Feels Right to Me': Inside Harvey Weinstein's Other Nightmare." *Vanity Fair*, December 20, 2017. https://www.vanityfair.com/news/2017/12/harvey-weinstein-nightmare-finding-neverland-amfar-money.

Cooper, Brittney C. *Eloquent Rage: A Black Feminist Discovers Her Superpower*. New York: Picador, 2018.

Coscarelli, Joe, and Melena Ryzik. "Ryan Adams Dangled Success. Women Say They Paid a Price." *New York Times*, February 13, 2019. https://www.nytimes.com/2019/02/13/arts/music/ryan-adams-women-sex.html.

De Becker, Gavin. *The Gift of Fear: And Other Survival Signals That Protect Us from Violence*. New York: Dell Publishing, 1997.

Deraniyagala, Sonali. *Wave*. New York: Alfred A. Knopf, 2013.

De Vogue, Ariane. "#MeToo Will Have Staying Power, Ruth Bader Ginsburg Insists." *CNN*, February 12, 2018. https://www.cnn.com/2018/02/11/politics/ruth-bader-ginsburg-me-too-poppy-harlow/index.html.

Dickerson, Caitlin. "Hazing, Humiliation, Terror: Working While Female in Federal Prison." *New York Times*, November 17, 2018. https://www.nytimes.com/2018/11/17/us/prison-sexual-harassment-women.html.

Durana, Alieza. "The Sexual-Harassment Victims Who Can't Get to Court." *Atlantic*, October 8, 2018. https://www.theatlantic.com/ideas/archive/2018/10/year-metoo-not-everyones-protected-sexual-harassment/572329.

Editors of *The Cut*. "Anita Hill: Won, Even Though She Lost." *The Cut*, October 15, 2018. https://www.thecut.com/2018/10/women-and-power-chapter-one.html.

Engel, Beverly. *The Emotionally Abusive Relationship: How to Stop Being*

Abused and How to Stop Abusing. Hoboken, NJ: John Wiley and Sons, Inc., 2002.

Evans, Patricia. *The Verbally Abusive Relationship: How to Recognize It and How to Respond.* New York: Adams Media, 2010.

Fallon, Kevin. "Oprah Takes a Powerful Stand on 'Leaving Neverland' Controversy: 'This Moment Transcends Michael Jackson.'" *Daily Beast*, March 5, 2019. https://www.thedailybeast.com/oprah-takes -a-powerful-stand-on-leaving-neverland-controversy-this-moment -transcends-michael-jackson.

Farrow, Ronan. "As Leslie Moonves Negotiates His Exit from CBS, Six Women Raise New Assault and Harassment Claims." *New Yorker*, September 9, 2018. https://www.newyorker.com/news/news-desk /as-leslie-moonves-negotiates-his-exit-from-cbs-women-raise-new -assault-and-harassment-claims.

Farrow, Ronan, and Jane Mayer. "Four Women Accuse New York's Attorney General of Physical Abuse." *New Yorker*, May 7, 2018. https:// www.newyorker.com/news/news-desk/four-women-accuse-new -yorks-attorney-general-of-physical-abuse.

Federal Bureau of Investigation. "Table 33: Ten-Year Arrest Trends." FBI: Uniform Crime Reporting, 2017. https://ucr.fbi.gov/crime-in-the-u.s. -/2017/crime-in-the-u.s.-2017/topic-pages/tables/table-33.

Fernandez, Manny. "'You Have to Pay with Your Body': The Hidden Nightmare of Sexual Violence on the Border." *New York Times*, March 3, 2019. https://www.nytimes.com/2019/03/03/us/border-rapes -migrant-women.html.

Fessler, Leah. "Tarana Burke, Creator of Me Too, Believes You Don't Have to Sacrifice Everything for a Cause." *Quartz*, February 6, 2018. https://qz.com/work/1193569/me-too-movement-creator-tarana -burke-says-you-dont-have-to-sacrifice-everything-for-a-cause.

Feuer, Alan. "Lawyer for 2 Schneiderman Accusers Brought Their Claims to Michael Cohen." *New York Times*, May 11, 2018. https://www .nytimes.com/2018/05/11/nyregion/eric-schneiderman-michael -cohen.html.

———. "Schneiderman Will Not Face Criminal Charges in Abuse Complaints." *New York Times*, November 8, 2018. https://www.nytimes .com/2018/11/08/nyregion/eric-schneiderman-abuse-charges .html.

Garcia-Moreno, Claudia, Alessandra Guedes, and Wendy Knerr. "Intimate Partner Violence," in *Understanding and Addressing Violence Against Women*, ed. Sarah Ramsay. Geneva: World Health Organization, 2012.

http://apps.who.int/iris/bitstream/10665/77432/1/WHO_RHR
_12.36_eng.pdf.

Goodyear, Dana. "Can Hollywood Change Its Ways?" *New Yorker*, January 1, 2018. https://www.newyorker.com/magazine/2018/01/08/can
-hollywood-change-its-ways.

Hakim, Danny, and William K. Rosenbaum. "New York's Attorney General in Battle with Trump." *New York Times*, December 16, 2017. https://www.nytimes.com/2017/12/26/nyregion/eric-schneiderman
-attorney-general-new-york.html.

Harwood, Erika. "Sally Field Shares Details from Her Controlling Relationship with Burt Reynolds." *Vanity Fair*, September 18, 2018. https://www.vanityfair.com/style/2018/09/sally-field-memoir-burt
-reynolds-relationship.

Hayek, Salma. "Harvey Weinstein Is My Monster Too." *New York Times*, December 12, 2017. https://www.nytimes.com/interactive/2017/12
/13/opinion/contributors/salma-hayek-harvey-weinstein.html.

Heilbrun, Carolyn G. *Writing a Woman's Life*. New York: W. W. Norton and Company, Inc., 1988.

Hill, Anita. "Anita Hill: Let's Talk About How to End Sexual Violence." *New York Times*, May 9, 2019. https://www.nytimes.com/2019/05
/09/opinion/anita-hill-sexual-violence.html.

———. "Anita Hill: How to Get the Kavanaugh Hearings Right." *New York Times*, September 18, 2018. https://www.nytimes.com/2018/09
/18/opinion/anita-hill-brett-kavanaugh-clarence-thomas.html.

Hod, Itay. "Anita Hill Calls on Hollywood to Make 'Tangible Commitments' to Address Harassment and Equality Goals." *The Wrap*, October 8, 2018. https://www.thewrap.com/anita-hill-calls-hollywood-make
-tangible-commitments-address-harassment-equality-goals.

Hunt, Elle. "'20 Minutes of Action': Father Defends Stanford Student Son Convicted of Sexual Assault." *Guardian*, June 5, 2016. https://www
.theguardian.com/us-news/2016/jun/06/father-stanford-university
-student-brock-turner-sexual-assault-statement.

Katersky, Aaron, Josh Margolin, and Justin Doom. "NY Attorney General Eric Schneiderman Resigns After Report He Abused 4 Women." *ABC News*, May 8, 2018. https://abcnews.go.com/Politics/york-attorney
-general-resign-reports-abuse-women/story?id=55002677.

Katzenberg, Lauren. "40 Stories from Women About Life in the Military." *New York Times*, March 8, 2019. https://www.nytimes.com/2019/03
/08/magazine/women-military-stories.html.

Langmuir, Molly. "What's Next for *New Yorker* Reporter Jane Mayer?" *Elle*,

February 27, 2019. https://www.elle.com/culture/a26537529/jane
-mayer-new-yorker-interview-kavanaugh.

Lithwick, Dahlia. "Rob Porter's History of Domestic Abuse Wasn't a Secret.
It's Just That No One Cared." *Slate*, February 8, 2018. https://slate
.com/news-and-politics/2018/02/rob-porters-history-of-domestic
-abuse-wasnt-a-secret.html.

MacKinnon, Catharine A. "#MeToo Has Done What the Law Could Not."
New York Times, February 4, 2018. https://www.nytimes.com/2018
/02/04/opinion/metoo-law-legal-system.html.

———. "Where #MeToo Came From, and Where It's Going." *The Atlantic*,
March 24, 2019. https://www.theatlantic.com/ideas/archive/2019/03
/catharine-mackinnon-what-metoo-has-changed/585313.

Maxouris, Christina. "R. Kelly Docuseries Leaves Behind a Burning Question: Do Black Girls' Lives Matter?" *CNN*, January 7, 2019. https://
www.cnn.com/2019/01/07/entertainment/r-kelly-celebrities-react
-on-docuseries/index.html.

Mayer, Jane. "The Case of Al Franken." *New Yorker*, July 22, 2019. https://
www.newyorker.com/magazine/2019/07/29/the-case-of-al-franken.

McArdle, Megan. "I Went Back to a Man Who Hit Me. I'm Still Thinking
About Why." *Washington Post*, May 8, 2018. https://www.washingtonpost
.com/opinions/i-went-back-to-the-man-who-hit-me-why/2018/05/08
/0acb4c54-52f2-11e8-abd8-265bd07a9859_story.html.

McIntosh, Jess. "I Went on a Date With Eric Schneiderman. It Took Me
Years to Process What Happened That Night." *Elle*, May 31, 2018.
https://www.elle.com/culture/a20896599/eric-schneiderman-date
-story-jess-mcintosh.

Méndez Berry, Elizabeth. "Street Harassment: The Uncomfortable Walk
Home." *Crunk Feminist Collective*, September 16, 2010. https://www
.crunkfeministcollective.com/2010/09/16/street-harassment-the
-uncomfortable-walk-home.

Meyer, Eileen Hoenigman. "How to Deal When a Colleague Is Threatened
by You." *Glassdoor*, May 11, 2018. https://www.glassdoor.com/blog
/threatened.

Miller, Chanel. *Know My Name: A Memoir*. New York: Viking, 2019.

Morgan, Richard. "Ken Friedman, Spotted Pig Owner, Steps Down After Sexual Harassment Accusations." *Time Out*, December 12, 2017.
https://www.timeout.com/newyork/news/ken-friedman-spotted-pig
-owner-steps-down-after-sexual-harassment-accusations-121217.

Morris, David J. *The Evil Hours: A Biography of Post-Traumatic Stress*. New
York: Eamon Dolan Books, 2015.

Myerson, Harold. "The Man the Banks Fear Most." *The American Prospect*, April 23, 2012. https://prospect.org/api/amp/power/man-banks-fear.

National Coalition Against Domestic Violence. "National Statistics." https://ncadv.org/statistics (accessed October 7, 2019).

Noah, Trevor. "Eric 'Champion of Women' Schneiderman Falls to Me Too Movement." Comedy Central, May 8, 2018. Video, 5:22. http://www.cc.com/video-clips/930keb/the-daily-show-with-trevor-noah-eric—champion-of-women—schneiderman-falls-to-the-me-too-movement.

Prokop, Andrew. "The Rob Porter Scandal Keeps Getting Worse for Trump's White House." *Vox*, February 9, 2018. https://www.vox.com/policy-and-politics/2018/2/8/16988560/rob-porter-allegations-resigns.

RAINN. "Scope of the Problem: Statistics." 2019. https://www.rainn.org/statistics/scope-problem (accessed October 7, 2019).

Ravitz, Jessica, and Arman Azad. "Memories That Last: What Sexual Assault Survivors Remember and Why." *CNN*, September 21, 2018. https://www.cnn.com/2018/09/21/health/memory-sexual-assault-ptsd/index.html.

Reiner, Andrew. "Boy Talk: Breaking Masculine Stereotypes." *New York Times*, October 24, 2018. https://www.nytimes.com/2018/10/24/well/family/boy-talk-breaking-masculine-stereotypes.html.

Remnick, David. "A Reckoning with Women Awaits Trump." *New Yorker*, February 11, 2018. https://www.newyorker.com/news/daily-comment/a-reckoning-with-women-awaits-trump.

———. "The Weinstein Moment and the Trump Presidency." *New Yorker*, November 20, 2017. https://www.newyorker.com/magazine/2017/11/20/the-weinstein-moment-and-the-trump-presidency.

Richards, Cecile. *Make Trouble: Stand Up, Speak Out, and Find the Courage to Lead*. New York: Simon and Schuster, 2018.

Schneiderman, Eric. "Transforming the Liberal Checklist." *The Nation*, February 21, 2008. https://www.thenation.com/article/transforming-liberal-checklist.

Schreckinger, Ben. "New York Attorney General Eric Schneiderman on What It Takes to Keep Trump in Check." *GQ*, November 29, 2017. https://www.gq.com/story/new-york-attorney-general-eric-schneiderman-trump-interview.

Schulman, Sarah. *Conflict Is Not Abuse: Overstating Harm, Community Responsibility, and the Duty of Repair*. Vancouver, Canada: Arsenal Pulp Press, 2016.

Shwayder, Maya. "A Same-Sex Domestic Violence Epidemic Is Silent." *Atlantic*, November 5, 2013. https://www.theatlantic.com/health /archive/2013/11/a-same-sex-domestic-violence-epidemic-is-silent /281131.

Scott, Dylan. "Read Christine Blasey Ford's Written Testimony: 'I Am Here Today Not Because I Want to Be. I Am Terrified.'" *Vox*, September 27, 2018. https://www.vox.com/2018/9/26/17907462/christine -blasey-ford-testimony-brett-kavanaugh-hearing.

Selvaratnam, Tanya. "What Happened After I Shared My Story of Abuse by New York's Attorney General." *New York Times*, October 6, 2018. https://www.nytimes.com/2018/10/06/opinion/sunday/eric -schneiderman-abuse.html.

Siemaszko, Corky. "For Decades, a Sexual Predator Doctor Groomed This Community to Believe He Could Do No Wrong." *NBC News*, March 17, 2019. https://www.nbcnews.com/news/us-news/decades -sexual-predator-doctor-groomed-community-believe-he-could-do -n982131.

Snyder, Emma M., Han Yan M. Chang, and Tracy J. Shors. "Stressful Life Memories Relate to Ruminative Thoughts in Women with Sexual Violence History, Irrespective of PTSD." *Frontiers in Psychiatry*, September 5, 2018. https://www.frontiersin.org/articles/10.3389/fpsyt .2018.00311/full.

Snyder, Rachel Louise. *No Visible Bruises: What We Don't Know About Domestic Violence Can Kill Us*. New York: Bloomsbury Publishing, 2019.

Sorkin, Andrew Ross. "Does a Lawsuit Now Help the Weinstein Victims?" *New York Times*, February 12, 2018. https://www.nytimes.com/2018 /02/12/business/dealbook/weinstein-victims-lawsuit.html.

Stark, Evan. *Coercive Control: How Men Entrap Women in Personal Life*. New York: Oxford University Press, 2007.

Tillet, Salamishah, and Scheherazade Tillet. "After the 'Surviving R. Kelly' Documentary, #MeToo Has Finally Returned to Black Girls." *New York Times*, February 2, 2019. https://www.nytimes.com/2019/01 /10/opinion/r-kelly-documentary-metoo.html.

Tolentino, Jia. "E. Jean Carroll's Accusation Against Donald Trump, and the Raising, and Lowering, of the Bar." *New Yorker*, June 25, 2019. https:// www.newyorker.com/news/our-columnists/e-jean-carrolls-accusation -against-donald-trump-and-the-raising-and-lowering-of-the-bar.

Traister, Rebecca. *Good and Mad: The Revolutionary Power of Women's Anger*. New York: Simon and Schuster, 2018.

Tsoulis-Reay, Alexa. "Here's How Consent and BDSM Role-Play Actually Work." *The Cut*, May 9, 2018. https://www.thecut.com/2018/05/how -to-role-play-bdsm-for-beginners.html.

Twohey, Megan. "Tumult After AIDS Fundraiser Supports Harvey Weinstein Production." *New York Times*, September 23, 2017. https://www. nytimes.com/2017/09/23/nyregion/harvey-weinstein-charity.html.

Valenti, Jessica. "Why Domestic Abusers Thrive in Trump's White House." *Guardian*, February 9, 2018. https://www.theguardian.com /commentisfree/2018/feb/09/why-domestic-abusers-trump-white -house.

Vulture Editors. "Samantha Bee and the *Full Frontal* Team Reflect on Their Wild Ride Since the Election." *Vulture*, August 24, 2018. http://www .vulture.com/2018/08/samantha-bee-full-frontal-vulture-fest.html.

Wang, Amy B. "'Complicit' Is the 2017 Word of the Year, According to Dictionary.com." *Washington Post*, November 27, 2017. https://www .washingtonpost.com/news/the-intersect/wp/2017/11/27/complicit -is-the-2017-word-of-the-year-according-to-dictionary-com.

Weitzman, Susan. *"Not to People Like Us": Hidden Abuse in Upscale Marriages.* New York: Basic Books, 2000.

Whipp, Glenn. "A Year After #MeToo Upended the Status Quo, the Accused Are Attempting Comebacks—But Not Offering Apologies." *Los Angeles Times*, October 5, 2018. http://www.latimes.com /entertainment/la-ca-mn-me-too-men-apology-20181005-story .html.

Williams, Terry Tempest. *When Women Were Birds: Fifty-four Variations on Voice.* New York: Picador, 2012.

Williams, Trey. "Former Weinstein Exec David Glasser Launches New 101 Studios." *The Wrap*, January 22, 2019. https://www.thewrap.com/former -weinstein-exec-david-glasser-launches-new-company-101-studios.

Willoughby, Jennie. "Jennie Willoughby: 'President Trump Will Not Diminish My Truth.'" *Time*, February 11, 2018. http://time.com /5143589/rob-porter-ex-wife-trump-domestic-violence.

World Health Organization. *WHO: Addressing Violence Against Women: Key Achievements and Priorities.* Geneva: World Health Organization, 2018. http://apps.who.int/iris/bitstream/handle/10665/275982 /WHO-RHR-18.18-eng.pdf?ua=1.

———. "Violence by Intimate Partners," in *World Report on Violence and Health*, eds. Etienne G. Krug, Linda L. Dahlberg, James A. Mercy, Anthony B. Zwi, and Rafael Lozano. Geneva: World Health

Organization, 2002. http://www.who.int/violence_injury_prevention /violence/global_campaign/en/chap4.pdf.

Zacharek, Stephanie, Eliana Dockterman, and Haley Sweetland Edwards. "The Silence Breakers." *Time*, December 6, 2017. http://time.com /time-person-of-the-year-2017-silence-breakers.

ABOUT THE AUTHOR

Tanya Selvaratnam is the author of *The Big Lie: Motherhood, Feminism, and the Reality of the Biological Clock*. Her work has been published in the *New York Times*, *Vogue*, *CNN*, *Glamour*, and *McSweeney's*, and she has been a fellow at Yaddo and Blue Mountain Center. She is an Emmy-nominated and Webby-winning filmmaker who has produced for Aubin Pictures, *Glamour* Women of the Year, Planned Parenthood, and the Vision & Justice Project.